M000234124

"I have often thought it was ri: congregation as 'the minister' to place 'the work of the minist. Christ. For this reason and more, *Every Waking Hour* is a gift to us all one hundred times over. Strickland and Quinn remind us that our job descriptions cannot ultimately be written on cards, etched into name plates, or affixed to email signatures. They are given by God for the world's good and God's glory. This book casts a compelling vision for vocation that is relevant to any believer with breath in their lungs and it arrives not a moment too soon."

Jonathan Merritt
author of *Jesus Is Better Than You Imagined*,
contributing writer for *The Atlantic*

"*Every Waking Hour* shows that God's calling and power in all of our lives, not just in church, is one of the deep patterns running through Scripture from beginning to end. Every Christian needs to see how this story is essential to the gospel story itself. Well done!"

Greg Forster
director of the Oikonomia Network
at Trinity International University

"Humans were created for work. It's a shame so many Christians don't know how to approach our work—and other vocations—as a key component of our faith. I'm thankful my friends Benjamin Quinn and Walter Strickland have written this timely book. I recommend it as an excellent primer on the Christian understanding of work and calling. I pray the Lord uses it to help us think rightly about God and his world and to pursue our callings in ways that glorify his name, advance his kingdom, and contribute to human flourishing."

Nathan A. Finn
dean of the School of Theology and Missions,
Union University

"*Every Waking Hour* dispels the 'hierarchy of callings' myth that is so pervasive in the church today. Striking a unique balance between the theological and the practical, this book is a must-read!"

Jordan Raynor
founder and CEO of Vocreo

"*Every Waking Hour* is a warm and engaging introduction to the proper place of work in Christian life. Quinn and Strickland give a clear overview of the intrinsic value of work in the Bible and its relationship to mission, along with a practical framework for putting theology into practice in churches."

Rev. Dr. Lyndon Drake
World Evangelical Alliance Council for Business and Theology

"The sacred-secular dualism born of reductionist gospel has crippled the church's mission to make known the good news that God is renewing all things including all of human cultural life. It is encouraging to see more and more folk in the church, especially the younger generation, waking up to creation-wide breadth of God's restoration. In this book, Benjamin Quinn and Walter Strickland clearly articulate the foundational biblical case that every waking hour belongs to Lord Christ. This book is well-written and rooted deeply in Scripture. It is an excellent introduction to the subject and could be used in a variety of settings to equip the laity for the calling to be a preview of the coming kingdom."

Michael W. Goheen
coauthor of *The Drama of Scripture*

"*Every Waking Hour* will help believers see their work, vocation, volunteerism, rest, and leisure as integral parts of the display of the kingdom of Christ in the spheres of man. Erasing the false dichotomy between sacred and secular callings, this work offers a redemptive-historical message that frames each believer's daily activities within the mission of Christ to the nations. Quinn and Strickland bring Ephesians 4:12 to life!"

Eric C. Redmond
assistant professor of Bible,
Moody Bible Institute, Chicago

EVERY WAKING HOUR

An Introduction to
Work and Vocation for Christians

EVERY WAKING HOUR

An Introduction to
Work and Vocation for Christians

Benjamin T. Quinn
&
Walter R. Strickland II

LEXHAM PRESS

Southeastern
Baptist Theological Seminary

Every Waking Hour: An Introduction to Work and Vocation for Christians

Lexham Press, 1313 Commercial St., Bellingham, WA 98225
LexhamPress.com

Print ISBN 9781577996781
Digital ISBN 9781577996798

Lexham Editorial: Rebecca Brant, Abigail Stocker
Cover Design: Christine Gerhart
Back Cover Design: Brittany Schrock
Typesetting: ProjectLuz.com

To Eugene Smith

TABLE OF CONTENTS

ACKNOWLEDGMENTS

We wish to thank Brannon Ellis at Lexham Press for believing in this project and Amy Whitfield at Southeastern Baptist Theological Seminary for her continued encouragement as the project came together. We would also like to thank Greg Forster of the Kern Family Foundation and their support of the Economic Wisdom Project, whose passion is to help connect pastors with faith, work, and economics. In addition, we would like to thank Devin Maddox for helping shape the book's content—originally taught in a seminary classroom—to be accessible to a broader audience.

We are grateful for the leadership of Danny Akin and Bruce Ashford, who have impressed upon our faculty, staff, and students that *every square inch* of the earth is the Lord's. We are grateful for others in the Southeastern family, and we owe undying appreciation to Billie Goodenough for offering her keen editorial eye to the entire project, and to Carrie Kelly and Justin Clark for their assistance as well. We would like to thank the students in our fall 2014 doctrine of vocation course, whose questions helped bring clarity to our ideas.

Finally, we would like to thank our wives for their continued excitement and encouragement throughout the project and for the sacrifices they made for this book to be completed. Ashley and Stephanie, thank you for allowing us to burn the midnight oil wrestling with these ideas, daydreaming about the book's content, and for being the guinea pigs for many of the ideas we present.

We pray that the efforts taken to produce this little book would allow God's people to transform their work from a dreaded task to a life-giving vocation for the kingdom's sake.

*Here is incontrovertible evidence that the New Testament
envisages ministry not as the prerogative of a clerical élite
but as the privileged calling of all the people of God. Thank
God that in our generation this biblical vision of an "every-
member ministry" is taking a firm hold in the church.*[1]

—JOHN R. W. STOTT, *The Message of Ephesians*

The Pulpit-Pew Divide

My (Benjamin's) older brother, Brandon, serves as princi-
pal of the public high school from which we both gradu-
ated. He recently told me a story about a kid we'll call Cory
who was in and out of Brandon's office for reasons mostly
related to drug possession. As Brandon questioned Cory
about the situation, he discovered Cory's problem wasn't
drug use—it was his family.

Cory's parents were using him to deliver drugs to another kid at school, who then delivered them to his own parents.
Their logic was that if Cory got caught, his punishment, as a

minor, would be minimal. If they got caught, it would likely entail jail time. In other words, lower risk for him than for them.

In one emotional conversation with Cory, Brandon asked, "Do you want out of this?" With teary eyes, Cory said, "Show me how! There ain't no way out of this!"

After Brandon shared this story with me, he asked about my job as a college and seminary professor: "What do you do every day?" I told him about various theology courses and students preparing for pastoral ministry and mission work. I also expressed my great delight in my work despite its challenges.

Less than three minutes after telling me about Cory, Brandon said, with all sincerity, "I just don't see how what I do is as important as what pastors, missionaries, or seminary professors do."

My jaw dropped, and my heart broke. How could Brandon conclude that his work is less valuable than mine? The question was a turning point.

I was immediately gripped by the gravity of Paul's words that apostles, prophets, evangelists, shepherds, and teachers are gifted "to equip the saints for the work of ministry, for building up the body of Christ" (Eph 4:12). And I was awakened to the problem of the pulpit-pew divide—the centuries-old chasm between those who occupy the pulpit and those who occupy the pew. The physical space between pulpit and pew in worship spaces is necessary for practical reasons. The metaphorical space between the "ordained" and the "ordinary" in the church, however, is unfortunate and unbiblical.

Every-Member Ministry

Ephesians 4:12 is the driving force behind this book. In this verse, Paul disrupts a misconception that is common among contemporary Christians—namely, that the ordained among us do the work of ministry. Is it true that those who receive a paycheck from a local church or Christian non-profit do ministry? Of course.

The problem, however, is in assuming that they are the *only* people in ministry or that *their* ministry—or work—is more important than anyone else's.

We argue that *every* Christ-follower is a minister by virtue of his or her relationship to God and the world around them. This stance is not merely an attempt to make Christians who do not work in full-time ministry feel valued—although they certainly are. It's a case for an "every-member ministry"—especially *at work*. Further, it's a biblical, theological, and practical framework for how to *understand* your work as ministry and then *execute* your work in fulfillment of the Great Commandment to love God and your neighbor.

In chapter 1, we provide a plan for a theology of work. We define "work" and "vocation" and consider how the two relate. Further, we explain why your work matters and how it contributes to God's work in the world.

Chapters 2 and 3 survey work and vocation in both the Old and New Testament. These chapters in particular attend to the various genres and broad contours of the Bible to provide a general sense for how work and vocation are understood throughout.

Chapter 4 asks, "What does it mean to work wisely in this world?" It addresses the relationship between Christ and wisdom, wisdom in (not of) the world, the way of wisdom, and wisdom at work.

Chapter 5 seeks to put it all together by weaving the key themes of kingdom, culture, and mission into the overall tapestry of the book.

Following a brief conclusion, we include an appendix that considers, "With whom should we work?" Here, we provide a structure for thinking about missional and moral collaboration with people from other denominations and/ or other faiths.[2] Other appendices include a set of questions for thinking through work and vocation as well as a list of recommended resources.

We pray that this book will alert God's people to the reality that every Christian wears a clerical collar. Paul taught us that anyone who is "in Christ … is a new creation (2 Cor 5:17). But let us not neglect what he said next: "All this is from God, who through Christ reconciled us to himself and gave us the ministry of reconciliation" (2 Cor 5:18). In light of this, all God's people must be intentional in joining our work with God's work of making all things new.

The FedEx logo is renowned among graphic designers. It has collected numerous awards and was selected as one of the eight best logos at the 35th anniversary of *Rolling Stone* magazine.[3] Using negative space and simple fonts, Lindon

Leader, the logo's creator, has created inconspicuously unforgettable graphics.

After being hired by Federal Express to create a new logo, Leader generated several potential designs, began to toy with the fonts, and stripped away clutter from each draft. His eye zeroed in on a particular design that abbreviated the company's name to FedEx because an arrow emerged between the E and the X. Mixing his two favorite fonts, the arrow became clearer, and the FedEx logo was born. After seeing the new FedEx graphic several times, Leader told his young daughter about the hidden arrow. Her eyes lit up, and she never saw the logo the same way again.

In the same way, we hope this book is the catalyst for an "aha moment" that allows you to see your work differently, whether you've been on the job for two months or two decades.[4] Unlocking the relationship between faith and work doesn't require a PhD. It's unlikely that you will discover any secret knowledge in this book that will give you the leg up in your workplace (or wherever you spend the majority of your time). Rather, it's our hope that you will begin to see connections between ideas you may have never imagined are related but in fact are. We hope it will be your "aha moment" in regards to your work.

CHAPTER 1

Theology of Work

We spend the vast majority of our waking hours on the job, yet glorifying God in our work is rarely a topic of conversation in the church. Faithful Christians who desire to honor God with their vocational lives often do so by working ethically, starting lunchtime Bible studies, facilitating a prayer time, or sharing their faith regularly. While each of these activities are honoring to God, he also cares about the *tasks* of our job as well.

Christ-followers who seek to integrate their faith into their work often stop just short of tapping into the essence of their vocation and, as a result, function like a chaplain on the job site, primarily meeting spiritual needs.

What Is Work?

What do we mean when we say "work" and "vocation"? Although these terms are often used interchangeably, in this book we will use them as defined below.

Work is what creatures do with God's creation.[1]

Is that broad? Yes, but think about it: When I walked into my office this morning, did "work" happen when I flipped on the light switch, pulled out my laptop, answered the first email, or sat down to start writing? We might say work began when I started doing something that pertained to my paycheck. But I've never received a paycheck for cutting my grass, and we can all agree that's work.

So where does work take place? Wherever people interact with God's world—whether planting bulbs or planting churches, raising children at home or driving to the office, writing a song or writing an amicus brief—it is all work.

Further, we understand work as inherently *good*. In Genesis 1–2, God gave work to Adam and Eve as part of their image-bearing opportunity and responsibility before sin entered into the picture. After the fall in Genesis 3, however, work neither stopped nor was rendered bad. Work remained good as God designed it, though it became difficult and painful and leaned away from God's intended ends; via misdirection, it tends away from God's original ends. Work now works against God's creatures in many ways. In addition to our labor, then, we must attend to the toilsome task of redirecting all things back to God through our work—yes, all things!

Does it feel a bit overwhelming? Indeed it does, but in Christ and by the Spirit, we join God in restoring all things to him, things both seen and unseen, which injects meaning and purpose into everything we do, from coaching to dog-walking.

Vocation is the way or ways in which we make ourselves useful to others.[2]

First, notice the term "others" in this definition. People were not created to live for self. We were created to live for others. The first "other" is God himself. This is why the Great Commandment (Matt 22:36–40) begins with "love the Lord your God with all your heart and with all your soul and with all your mind." To begin any other way would be idolatry. But, as Jesus taught, the second is like the first; we are to "love your neighbor as yourself." "Self" simply serves as the pivot point from which we direct our love and energy upward, then outward.

Second, consider the words "way or ways" from our definition. The first thing to notice is the plural, "ways." Despite the grammar, "vocation" is not singular. Often when we hear the word "vocation" we immediately think of our place of employment, and indeed this is *a* vocation. But it isn't the only one. "Vocation" simply means "calling," and each of us inhabits multiple callings. For a Christian, the first and most important calling is to trust and obey Jesus. Through our union with him, we live out other callings in the arenas of family, church community, neighborhood, and occupation or place of employment. There may be more vocations for some, but likely not fewer.

Each of these arenas, then, is a vocation wherein we are called to love God and love others, though only one (for most people) provides a paycheck.

Work is the hand that animates the glove of vocation. Picture a leather glove lying on your kitchen table. For it to be useful, you must slip your hand inside. But you can't simply shove your hand into the glove however you choose; you must place each finger in the proper sleeve for the glove to be useful at all.

We should understand work and vocation as relating in a similar fashion. We are called to multiple arenas in life and, thus, to occupy multiple vocations. The proper way to work out our vocations is by always striving for the double love of God and neighbor. But these vocations do not exercise love for God and his world until we put on our vocational gloves and get to work.

To be sure, all work is vocational, but the doing of the work looks different in each vocation. Changing diapers at home is as much an exercise in double love of God and neighbor as is delivering meals on wheels, printing the bulletins at church, or spending extra time editing tomorrow's sports column. Each is important and demands our faithfulness.

Work and Creation

If work is what we do with God's creation, then we must understand creation to understand work. Scripture is the highest authority for our understanding of creation—and therefore serves as our source for understanding work and its connection with creation.

Creation

God created everything and declared that it was good (Gen 1:4, 10, 12, 18, 21, 25, 31). This affirmation dispels the notion of a sacred-secular divide (i.e., dualism), which implies that only part of creation is good. Dualistic thought subverts a Christian understanding of the workplace and divorces our faith from everyday tasks. In essence, dualism divides our allegiance and thwarts our ability to engage our work with kingdom-oriented single-mindedness. It draws a line through the world and forces us to walk on both sides of it, ultimately relegating spiritual matters to one side and vocational and other common concerns to the other.[3] In the end, a worldview divided into sacred and secular spheres undermines the teachings of Scripture (Gen 1; 1 Tim 4:4) and fails to recognize that the Christian life as a whole is dedicated to the Lord.

Humanity is the crowning jewel of creation, and God pronounced it to be "very good" (Gen 1:31). The essence of humanity's goodness is that we are image-bearers of God himself, which means that, like God, we exist in relationship to the things and people around us. Human existence is characterized by four relationships that illuminate the scope of redemption and demonstrate how our work furthers God's plan of redemption: relationship with God, with one another, with oneself, and with God's creation.

The Fall

At the fall in Genesis 3, a loving God gave Adam and Eve the ability to express their love for him by choosing to follow his commands or to pursue joy and fulfillment on their own—the decision to eat the fruit from the tree of knowledge. Adam and Eve chose to eat from the tree, and their sinful act of rebellion fractured the harmony that characterized all that God declared to be good, including humanity's fundamental relationships. Sin created a divide between man and God, strife between people, unrest within every individual, and disorder among God's creation.

Redemption

Every good story has a conflict and resolution, and Scripture is no exception. In the same chapter that chronicles the fall of humanity—the conflict—the biblical writer records the resolution—the beginning of God's plan for redemption. Genesis 3:15 declares, "I will put enmity between you and the woman, and between your offspring and her offspring; he shall bruise your head, and you shall bruise his heel." In short, this is the first proclamation of Christ's coming to restore all that God originally declared to be good.

Restoration

The Old Testament documents God faithfully keeping his promises to his people. One promise—the coming of the Son of David—was later fulfilled in Jesus (Matt 1:1). Christ's death and resurrection initiated an era in which the restorative power of the cross can be glimpsed throughout God's creation, including in our work. But God's work of redemption will culminate in a restoration of his Eden-like rule and reign only during his coming kingdom. The entire biblical drama moves toward this end.[4]

As the story unfolds, we work.

Why Your Work Matters to God

We cannot understand the conflict and resolution of the biblical drama without understanding the law. The Great Commandment is a wonderful summary of the law that contains two complementary axes. The first is vertical and highlights love of God: "You shall love the Lord your God with all your heart and with all your soul and with all your mind" (Matt 22:37). We usually think about the vertical dimension of the law in terms of worship or relationship with God. Unfortunately, the vertical dimension seldom overlaps with the horizontal.

The second is horizontal and underscores love of neighbor: "You shall love your neighbor as yourself" (Matt 22:39). We tend to regard the horizontal dimension as relationships or social justice. And, unfortunately, we seldom connect these areas of life with the vertical dimension of the law.

An overemphasis on the vertical dimension of the law with little regard for the horizontal can be caricatured as zealous Christian fundamentalism. Overemphasis on the horizontal dimension to the detriment of the vertical can be caricatured as liberal social gospel. Both pursuits are essential to participating in God's plan, but when one holds distinct priority over the other, it hinders our pursuit of the Great Commission. We must hold them together and in balance to be faithful to God in every area of our lives.

Throughout the history of the church, different Christian groups have favored the vertical or horizontal imperative of the Great Commandment. Generally speaking, theologically conservative Christians expend significant energy on loving God, and those who are more theologically liberal have historically focused on loving their neighbor.

The conservative Christian's faith is characterized by spiritual formation activities that focus on personal holiness, like Scripture memorization, daily devotions, prayer, fasting, solitude, and personal worship. When spiritually oriented believers look outward to engage the culture, their efforts are often evangelistic in scope, and their chief aim is to verbally proclaim the gospel—and so it is on the jobsite. Vertically oriented Christians strive to cultivate deep personal communion with God, and they desire the same for their coworkers. Consequently, their efforts are aimed at enabling their coworkers to participate in "things above."

In contrast, liberal Christians tend to see their mission as reaching out to their neighbors, to bring to earth the peace that characterizes God's future kingdom. As a result, their expressions of following Christ include pursuing liberation for the oppressed, ending classism, and eliminating hunger, to name a few. Horizontally oriented believers often seek to use their jobs to pursue admirable goals; however, if their efforts are divorced from the God whose Spirit grants transformative power, they become simply another humanitarian endeavor.

Looking to Christ as our example, we see the vertical and horizontal planes of the Christian life modeled beautifully; he demonstrated social concern *and* evangelistic passion. Despite the popularity of Matthew's Great Commission narrative, John's account holds both dimensions of a cruciform life in tension in semiveiled language. John 20:21 reads: "Jesus said to them again, 'Peace be with you. As the Father has sent me, even so I am sending you.'" Christ's challenge to his followers is to live a life modeled after him as he faithfully embodied the character of the Father, who sent him.

Contrary to popular understanding, every believer's restorative mission is the whole story of Scripture itself. We must give our attention to the entire biblical story to understand our mission in light of it.[5]

Our mission is tangled up in our vocation—not with our careers, salaries, or 401(k) plans. The vocations to which we are all called fit meaningfully somewhere into the arc of God's story.

The biblical narrative includes far more than the eradication of our sin problem and individual spirituality; it is about God's reign, rebellion from his rule, and creation regained for his glory.[6] Since we have defined work as what people do with creation, our vocation is an avenue to demonstrate Christ's rule now until it comes fully in his kingdom. Let's explore the biblical drama to better understand the role of our work in God's plan.

Work and Redemption

Christ-followers living between Christ's first and second coming have experienced the restorative fruit of the resurrection in our salvation, and we have been commissioned to both proclaim and demonstrate the kingdom that is to come. The words and deeds of God's people function as signposts or precursors to the reality of Christ's reign in the midst of a world that groans for redemption—and our work is essential to this testimony. In essence, the Christian's work, through his or her vocation, should be a seed of redemption that will bloom in God's forever kingdom.

Vertically oriented Christians operate with the working assumption that having a job affords them relational opportunities to serve their neighbors. The underlying principle here is that taking part in God's mission is entirely separate from their job description, and work is, at best, a setting for relationships in which they can proclaim the gospel. To take it a step further, cultivating creation as a witness to God's sustaining hand in the world is just as essential to our work for the sake of honoring God and serving our neighbor.

To illustrate how image-bearers emulate God's restorative work in creation, Robert J. Banks offers descriptions of six divine activities and pairs them with contemporary vocations in which God's people work as Christ's sustaining hand in creation.[7] First, Banks highlights God's saving and reconciling character and equates it with the work of evangelists, pastors, and counselors who mirror this divine activity, thus offering a glimpse of God's passion for reconciliation and hope for the future. Filmmakers, artists, songwriters, and storytellers can also incorporate messages and symbols into their work that focus our gaze on God the reconciler.

We witness God's creative genius in his fashioning of the physical world in which we live. Those who work as construction workers, painters, and interior designers display craftsmanship that reflects divine creativity and beauty.

Furthermore, God's providential work of sustaining and ordering creation is captured by a set of vocations. Work that maintains order—like public policy, building inspection, and wildlife preservation—participates in the sustaining ministry of God in creation (Col 1:17).

Justice is essential to God's character, and judges, lawyers, paralegals, government regulators, law enforcement officers, and other types of advocates work to bring about the justice and peace that characterizes God and his kingdom (Deut 32:4; Job 37:23; Psa 89:14). Doctors, paramedics, social workers, and counselors are God's instruments in bringing compassion and healing to those in need (Exod 34:6; Psa 103:8). Through the Holy Spirit, God enlightens people to truth (1 Cor 2:10–11), and teachers, writers, pastors, and journalists take part in this divine work as well.

Conclusion

Each day we have openings to bear witness to the gospel of Jesus Christ. Take every opportunity to demonstrate the full scope of the good news, especially where you spend most of your time working. If we fail to do so in the majority of our lives, it's reasonable to conclude we have failed to understand what it means to integrate the gospel fully into our lives to any meaningful extent. Christ-followers are new creations, and we are simultaneously aware of sin's grip on creation and the overcoming power of God's redemptive plan. Christians—those inwardly transformed by the gospel—are equipped by the Spirit to proclaim and demonstrate God's desire to reclaim his pre-fall relationship with humanity and to extend his love to their neighbors in their work.

Action Points

- In what ways has dualism (separating the spiritual and physical) shaped how you view your work?

- How can you intentionally love both God and your neighbor on the job?

- What aspects of your work contain elements of the gospel story, and how can you use those elements to proclaim Christ?

- Is it important for us to share the gospel at work? Is it more important that we excel in our work? Or are both priorities?

Recommended Reading

DeKoster, Lester. *Work: The Meaning of Your Life*. Grand Rapids: Christian's Library Press, 2010.

Keller, Timothy. *Every Good Endeavor*. New York: Dutton, 2012.

Wright, Christopher J. H. *The Mission of God: Unlocking the Bible's Grand Narrative*. Downers Grove, IL: IVP Academic, 2006.

CHAPTER 2

Work throughout the Old Testament

So, in the world that Westerners usually think of as the cradle of our philosophy and our culture, work, manual labor especially, was considered beneath a man's dignity, and was usually relegated to slaves or to the culturally lowest dregs of freemen. Labor was no activity for the educated and the cultured. Scripture, on the other hand, paints a very different picture.[1]

—CHAD BRAND, *Flourishing Faith*

The song "Livin' for the Weekend" was made and remade because it resonated with the American workforce. Each Monday, laborers punch the clock with the thrill of the weekend behind them and the dread of another workweek ahead. For many, five of seven days each week are a necessary evil, endured to pay the bills arising from a weekend of leisure. Many workers dream of becoming wealthy enough to escape the rigors and monotony of the workplace. For them, work is a curse to be escaped.

The absence of biblical teaching on work, combined with common cultural misconceptions about work's value and role, result in a miserable workforce that labors for all the wrong reasons. Although the tide is changing, many Westerners work almost solely to make an income. In this paradigm, we define success by our ability to earn money and sustain a particular lifestyle. Working primarily for pay has led people to lucrative careers that leave them unfulfilled without their knowing why. Could they be more fulfilled in another job? Is all work cursed and therefore miserable?

The Word of God is authoritative in every area of life, including our work. Scripture reminds us of its usefulness for teaching, rebuke, correction, and training in righteousness, so that every one of God's servants may be thoroughly equipped for every good work (2 Tim 3:16–17). Christians have a tendency either to read Scripture from a temporal perspective, which jettisons its spiritual imperatives, or from a spiritual point of view, which separates the spiritual realities from their daily implications.

Each part of the Old Testament (the Law [the first five books of the Bible], Historical Books, Poetic Books, and Prophetic Books) contributes to its teaching on work. The first three chapters of Genesis begin laying a foundation for a biblical view of work that helps inject new meaning into whatever we put our hands to (Eccl 9:10).

God at Work (Genesis 1–3)

The dream of a life without work is nothing new. Ancient Greek philosophers believed that gods were perfect minds, uninvolved with the daily concerns of this world. These philosophers sought to become like their gods by eliminating common worldly cares in favor of contemplating otherworldly ideals. In contrast to Greek thought—and much of contemporary Western thought—Scripture dispels the "work is bad" mentality.

Creation (Genesis 1–2)

The first scene of the biblical story depicts God hard at work. In contrasting the biblical God with Greek gods, David H. Jensen says, "God does not sit enthroned in heaven removed from work, willing things into existence by divine fiat. Unlike the gods of Greco-Roman mythologies, who absolve themselves of work ... the God of the Bible works."[2] From the outset of Scripture, God is creating (Gen 1:1), speaking (Gen 1:3, 6, 9, 11, 14, 20, 26), separating (Gen 1:4, 6), making (Gen 1:7, 26), and naming/calling (Gen 1:8, 10) his creation. Divine action recorded in the first chapter of Genesis dispels the notion that work is a result of the fall.

The Fall (Genesis 3)

God continued to work after humanity fell to sin. He was not asleep at the wheel, so to speak. God's work never ceased; he immediately began to pursue relationship with Adam and Eve when their sin led them to hide from him

(Gen 3:9). After announcing the curse on human work because of sin (Gen 3:14–19), God continued his redemptive work among humanity.

Redemption (Genesis 3)

With the work of his hands, God crafted garments for Adam and Eve that signified hope in the midst of toil and disorder (Gen 3:21). The coverings God provided were a sign of his divine protection from exposure to a sin-filled world. Ultimately hope and blessing would come through the one who would crush the head of the serpent (Gen 3:15), but God worked to heal Adam and Eve's immediate brokenness as well. In the same way, God's people should conduct their work to manifest the redemption that will be realized in the future.

Unless workers understand that God created work as good (Gen 1–2), that humans sinned and brought a curse upon their work, and that God cares about redeeming work and restoring his rule, then it's no wonder that some dread going to the office, the factory, the coffee shop. Unless workers understand their work in relationship to God, work doesn't make much sense of reality.

Workers in God's Image

Working as an image-bearer of God imports new meaning to our understanding of vocation. Timothy Keller notes that Adam and Eve's command to "fill the earth" is distinct from that given to the plants and animals; their task was to multiply and teem over the earth (Gen 1:11, 20–25).[3] Humanity was given the same task, but with the additional instruction to cultivate civilization with all of its organizational complexity. In essence, humanity is called to function as "small 'l' lords" over creation.[4]

The creation account records God's image-bearers emulating his divine actions much like we do in our work today. On the sixth day of creation, God intentionally refrained from dotting all the I's and crossing all the T's. In his wisdom, he left potential for the world to be developed further; in effect, his image-bearers are called to pick up where he left off. Adam's naming of the animals is one example of such work (Gen 1:19–20). That task mirrored the divine action of exercising dominion over creation by naming its elements (Gen 1:8), thereby bringing chaos into order (Gen 1:2).

Humanity's primary task is to develop civilization; that includes both social and cultural dimensions.[5] Building a society includes fashioning an economy, business practices, sports, art, cultural norms (like folkways and mores), music, and leisure. God establishes this potential in the beginning chapters of Genesis. We see only a glimpse in the garden, yet we continue this work today.

Fundamentally, the Genesis account makes it clear that continuing God's work of caring for and cultivation creation brings dignity to God's image-bearers; these are good and necessary acts for God's vice-regents on earth. In fact, exercising biblical dominion over creation not only instills dignity in humanity, it brings glory to God by upholding his creative design for work in his world. At the fall our concept of work was fractured, resulting in a myriad of problems. Overwork and slothfulness are distortions of God's rhythm of work and rest modeled in Genesis.

Overworking cuts against the pattern God inscribed into creation. In a Genesis 3 world, overworking as a means of finding significance is a symptom of misunderstanding how personal value is derived in our work. We work too much when we find an unhealthy degree of personal worth in the work itself and not in God, the giver of our ability to work. Overworking also indicates we have transferred the value of work from being an act of worship that honors God and loves neighbor to being an act of gaining profit .

Work and Rest

Rest allows us to reassign proper value to our work in a way that pleases the Lord. First, rest ensures that we do not become machine-like commodities, valuable only for the goods or services we produce. Rest expands our sense of personal value because we spend that time exercising different parts of our humanity. A proverb of unknown origin encourages us to seek a dignifying balance: "If you work with your mind, you must rest with your hands; if you work with your hands, you must rest with your mind."

Rest also recalibrates the market-drive values of the Western mind. German philosopher Josef Pieper touched on this in his essay "Leisure, the Basis of Culture." Keller summarizes Pieper's point thus:

> Leisure is not the mere absence of work, but an attitude of mind or soul in which you are able to contemplate and enjoy things as they are in themselves, without regard to their value or their immediate utility. The work-obsessed mind—as in our Western culture—tends to look at everything in terms of efficiency, value, and speed. But there must also be an ability to enjoy the most simple and ordinary aspects of life, even ones that are not strictly useful, but just delightful.[6]

In contrast, slothfulness distorts God's plan for humanity in a way that strips people of the opportunity for dignity. Although Genesis 1 does not directly admonish the sluggard, the implication is apparent. The book of Proverbs explicitly addresses the idler with deeply critical language. The lazy person is characterized as making outlandish excuses for not being vigilant in daily tasks, saying, "There is a lion outside! I shall be killed in the streets!" (Prov 22:13). The dullard is also described as groaning like a squeaky door when it's time to arise (Prov 26:14). Proverbs' most vivid word picture depicts the slothful as being too shiftless to follow through with what they've begun doing: "The sluggard buries his hand in the dish and will not even bring it back to his mouth" (Prov 19:24).

The creation account of Genesis lays the groundwork for understanding God's intent for work. God is a worker, and thus his image-bearers are workers and are dignified in so doing. The uniqueness of our work is as God's reflection in humanity, one that corrects misguided motivations for work and the common problems of over- and underworking. Let's look to Genesis 11 for additional instruction on God's understanding of work.

A Tale of Misplaced Glory (Genesis 11)

Genesis 11 is a popular text among linguists, missionaries, and anthropologists; it also makes an important contribution to our discussion about work. In the wake of Genesis 3, God's intent for his creation was fractured; Genesis 11 reveals humanity's heart-posture—they moved away from God. The Tower of Babel recounts people working with their hands for their own glory and personal gain; it also records God's response to their sin. The early verses of the chapter foreshadow the story's destructive outcome by noting the people's movement "from the east ... [to] a plain in the land of Shinar" (Gen 11:2). This phrase picks up on an existing theme in Genesis in which people leave God's good provision to provide for themselves by their own means (Gen 3:24; 4:16; 13:11).

Genesis 11:4 outlines the fourfold strategy developed by the people in Shinar: (1) building a tower (2) to make a name for themselves and (3) erecting a city (4) so they would not be scattered across the face of the earth. These ancient people are not unlike the 21st-century workforce—people who stop at nothing to make a name for ourselves. Building a tower to gain attention from surrounding peoples is much like burning the wick at both ends to be acknowledged on the job or shamelessly promoting your vocational achievements.

Using your God-given ability with the sole purpose of making a name for yourself contradicts God's plan in Scripture. From Genesis to Revelation, God's desire is to make *himself* known and thus further his plan to redeem the brokenness in the world. For example, the creation account illustrates that nothing and no one should rival God's rule. His creative action, recorded day by day, contrasts and undercuts the pagan deities of the ancient Near East. Likewise, God's passion for his renown is unmistakable in the Great Commission passages in the New Testament. God has granted us skill and abilities as a means of directing people to himself, and it is a disservice to our neighbors to use our God-given abilities as an opportunity for self-promotion instead of Christ-exaltation.

In the end, no matter how impressive your skills, God alone saves fallen humanity. John Piper says it well: "God is the one being in the universe for whom self-exaltation is the most loving act. Anyone else who exalts himself [or herself] distracts us from what we need, namely, God."[7] Curbing the tendency for self-promotion is a difficult task, especially when our hard work—done in the privacy of a study, shop, or lab—is finally recognized. The danger of self-promotion is that we rob God of his glory and distract people from the big-L Lord of the universe with our small-l lording over creation. If God affords you the opportunity to close a deal or get the contract, do your coworkers a favor and direct their attention to the God who created industry and enterprise.

God desires to use his people and their gifts for his glory, but he will not hesitate to discipline his children for deviating from his plan, as he did in Shinar. By his grace, God scattered the people in Shinar to remove them from patterns of temptation and distractions that plagued them (Gen 11:8). The God of redemption did not abandon those who were scattered because of their sin; he sent Abram and his descendants to restore them to a right relationship with him (Gen 12:1–3). The glory for our work belongs to God alone; be careful to direct those who respect your work to the original worker, God himself.

Work is addressed throughout the law. Lessons about work illustrate God's desire for his people to live for him and for each other. By upholding the statues of the law, the lives of God's people would emerge in contrast to those around them; those distinctions portray the character of the God on whose behalf they worked.

Faithfulness in Economic Difficulty (Ruth 1–2)

Within the Historical Books of the Bible (Joshua through Esther), Ruth displays the centrality of faithfulness, stewardship, and mercy from two distinct perspectives when working for the Lord. The story of Ruth is set in a time of a desperate famine that plagued a society dependent on agriculture (Ruth 1:1). Ruth carried the additional burdens of being without a husband or father-in-law in a patriarchal society (Ruth 1:3–5) and having to provide for herself and her mother-in-law as a foreigner in the land (Ruth 1:22).

Ruth's safety net crumbled beneath her feet, much like those in our cities today who stand on the street corner holding signs saying, "Need work, please help." During a very difficult season in her life, the Lord blessed Ruth as she exemplified faithfulness during economic and personal trials. Ruth's first step of faithfulness was to actively pursue a chance to work when it arose (Ruth 2:1-2). When given the opportunity, Ruth worked faithfully on the job and made the most of it (Ruth 2:7).

That her own and Naomi's needs were met was not due to Ruth's actions alone; her faithfulness was productive because Boaz chose to love God and his neighbor with his belongings. Boaz carefully stewarded his resources on behalf of another by taking the concept of gleaning (Lev 19:9-10) to heart. God's law instructed his people to love the sojourner and the poor as a reflection of his love for them. Boaz embodied this call when he invited Ruth to gather food from his fields (Ruth 2:8-9, 15-16). Moreover, Boaz went beyond the call of Leviticus 19 and protected Ruth when she was vulnerable (Ruth 2:8-9), honored her for her integrity (Ruth 2:10-11), and intentionally acted as a means of grace that pointed to her ultimate provider, God (Ruth 2:11-13).

We often associate stewardship with material commodities like finances and other resources. In this story, Boaz is an excellent steward of immaterial resources—namely his power and influence. Although people often abuse their positions of power and, thus, they often have negative connotations, we need to examine power and influence to better understand the essential elements of this dynamic.

Boaz owned a significant amount of land as well as having workers, access to crops, and significant financial resources. Like Boaz, everyone has some degree of power, be it small or great, but the question for each of us is the same: How do you steward your God-given influence? The Christian faith implores us to love God and neighbor by leveraging even the smallest amount of power on behalf of others.

Having mercy on those in poverty is part and parcel to the Christian message. As those who have some measure of influence, we are responsible to pursue opportunities to help the economically broken to flourish. Recall the four principles of robust Christian worldview noted in the introduction: a relationship with God, others, oneself, and God's creation. Material poverty arises as a symptom when one or more of these relationships becomes disproportionately strained. The gleaning model depicted in the book of Ruth offers an example for us today. Such scenarios offer a disenfranchised person a Christ-like example, an opportunity to forge new relationships, the dignity of working for a wage, and an opportunity to gain a marketable skill that could be useful for future employment.

The Virtuous Woman (Proverbs 31)

In contrast to the slothful worker mentioned in the section above, the virtuous woman is a sterling picture of work in the Poetic Books (Job through Song of Songs). The virtuous woman is presented as the personification of economic savvy and wisdom at the end of a book that implores readers to seek understanding. The word "economic" here is used in a broad sense, in reference to the web of relationships that people inhabit on a daily basis. For example, the virtuous woman inhabits three of Martin Luther's four vocational spheres—namely, family, workplace, and society.

Scripture highlights the completeness of the woman's wisdom in a 22-line acrostic poem that demonstrates her thoroughly wise ways from beginning to end (or from A to Z).[8] Thus, her example is far more than a checklist for men to impose on a potential spouse; she is an example of wise living for men and women alike, although she takes on the particularities of femininity and motherhood.

The virtuous woman demonstrates how wisdom informs action in our private and public lives. Her husband trusts her implicitly (Prov 31:11, 28); the poem's chiastic structure demonstrates how his success is wrapped up in hers (31:23). In addition, her children rise up and call her blessed because of her tireless care for them (31:28). The consistency of her character shines through the praise of those who know her most intimately.

The virtuous woman works wisely in every sphere she engages. Scripture explores the nature of her work in the home by noting that she rises early to provide food for her household (31:15). She does not fret about harsh weather conditions because she has prepared her home for every season (31:21–22). She's able to accomplish all of this because she does not drink from the cup of idleness (31:27).

The virtuous woman's diligence is not solely relegated to the home; her industrious spirit stimulates the economy inside and outside of the home in the marketplace (31:13–14).

Her business ventures include real estate, farming (31:16), sewing (31:19), and general business instincts (31:18). She is careful to turn her business acumen to the good of others as she ultimately loves God and her neighbors by looking after those who are in need (31:20).

In keeping with the message of Proverbs, the wisdom of the virtuous woman begins with fearing the Lord (9:10; 31:30). She provides a wonderful conclusion to the book of Proverbs and gives each of us a real-life example of wisdom in the workplace. We will further consider the importance of the virtuous woman in chapter 4.

A Prophet for Justice (Amos)

In contrast to Wisdom literature, which offers insights for the individual, the Prophetic Books deliver communal wisdom and warnings to God's people. The context in which Amos prophesied was characterized by injustice in the workplace: He paints a disturbing picture of a wealthy merchant class that enjoyed winter and summer homes adorned with ivory (Amos 3:15) at the expense of the poor.

Amos laments that the oppressed were denied justice due to the heavy taxes on grain (5:11), corruption in the judicial system (5:12), distortion of prices from the use of inaccurate weights (8:5), and a host of other matters that grieved the heart of God. Amos prophesied to warn Israel that their covenant violations would result in judgment.

In an effort to reform the injustices of the merchant class, Amos often refers to the Creator (4:13; 5:8; 9:6) to expose their actions as sins against him as well as against the neighbors they cheated. The people should have known better; God has inscribed creation with his wisdom and justice, and living against the grain of God's intent wounds both oppressor and oppressed.

The Israelites became so sly in their own minds that they tried to manipulate God just as they manipulated the poor. The merchants sought to use spiritual acts of worship in an effort to obligate God to bless them while neglecting the public and social implications of such acts. God lamented that he took no delight in their assemblies (5:21); he did not accept their grain offerings (5:22); and he did not look upon their sacrifices (5:22) or listen to their songs of worship (5:23). Instead he called for justice to roll down like waters and righteousness like an ever-flowing stream (5:24).

In thriving economies, God's stern response to injustice is especially important for the wealthy and powerful. In corporations that are not seeking to be like Christ, managers and executives tend to look after their own interests at the expense of their workers. Amos reminds us that abusing the lowly is not exercising autonomy in a free-market economy—it's sin.

The message of loving one's neighbor permeates the prophets. Jeremiah 29:7 is becoming a theme verse for those who desire to be a blessing to the community in which they live. The significance of this verse extends beyond "seeking the welfare of the city" to the reality that God's people were in exile. Exiled Israel was called to demonstrate the virtues prescribed in the law not just to other Israelites but to all people no matter where they lived; Israel's actions in the public square directly reflected on the God they served.

Conclusion

Each genre of the Old Testament contributes to the Bible's teaching on work. It is our hope that children will grow up reading not only the miraculous stories about crossing the Red Sea, David killing Goliath, and Jonah and the whale, but also stories about stewardship, justice, and flourishing in the workplace. After all, each of them is destined for some form of work, and we should help them rehearse how to work in a manner pleasing to God.

Action Points

- How do you regularly apply the principle of work and rest?

- How have you leveraged your God-given gifts for your own gain?

- What are some areas where God has given you influence, and how can you use it generously with others?

Recommended Reading

Bartholomew, Craig G., and Ryan P. O'Dowd. *Old Testament Wisdom Literature: A Theological Introduction.* Downers Grove, IL: InterVarsity Press, 2011.

Piper, John. *Don't Waste Your Life.* Wheaton, IL: Crossway, 2003.

Vos, Geerhardus. *Biblical Theology: Old and New Testaments.* Edinburgh: The Banner of Truth Trust, 1975.

Wolters, Albert. *Creation Regained: Biblical Basics for a Reformational Worldview.* Grand Rapids: Eerdmans, 2005.

CHAPTER 3

Work throughout the New Testament

No crooked table legs or ill-fitting drawers ever, I dare swear,
came out of the carpenter's shop at Nazareth. Nor, if they
did, could anyone believe that they were made by the same
hand that made Heaven and earth. No piety in the worker
will compensate for work that is not true to itself; for any
work that is untrue to its own technique is a living lie.[1]

—DOROTHY SAYERS, "Why Work?"

What does the New Testament say about work? The New Testament uses the terms "work" and "works."[2] The term "works" alarms the theological sensibilities of good Protestants. And indeed it should. The relationship of faith and works has a long, complex, and important history in the church. Our aim here is not to provoke the *"faith* and works" discussion, but instead to shape the *"work* and works" discussion.

Consider the words "mission" and "missions." In Christian circles, the term "missions" is often associated with trips, either domestic or abroad, dedicated to evangelizing a particular group of people. Sometimes this is accomplished by way of door-to-door or street evangelism, and other times it is coupled with service projects.

The word "mission," on the other hand, connotes something related but different. Mission is a bigger idea than missions. For Christians, mission relates to the broad purpose and direction of life, not just to dedicated trips.

The terms "work" and "works" share a similar relationship. "Work" is a bigger idea that encompasses everything people do with creation. "Works," though an integral idea for the New Testament, tends to get relegated to historical and theological discussions about the nature of Christian salvation. Also, "work" in the New Testament tends to signify the material, hands-on kind of work, whereas "works" often connotes a spiritual sense. The same Greek word is usually used for both, however, alerting us to the intertwined relationship between our physical and spiritual labors.

Further, understanding the relationship between works and faith is also important. Paul's words in Ephesians 2:8–10 help us here. He writes:

> For by grace you have been saved through faith. And this is not your own doing; it is the gift of God, not a result of works, so that no one may boast. For we are his workmanship—created in Christ Jesus for good works, which God

    prepared beforehand, that we should walk
    in them.

From this passage, would you say Paul is in favor of faith or works? I would argue that, for Paul, it isn't an either/or, it's a both/and—not faith *or* works, but faith *and* works. To be more precise, it's faith, *then* works.

We must be careful to emphasize both faith *and* works, and faith *then* works. All of this is critical to our understanding of work in the Christian life.

Work and Jesus

Before Jesus was known as the Christ, he was known as a carpenter. Consider the significance of that. Though the Scriptures tell us almost nothing about Jesus' life as a carpenter, it is nevertheless a significant part of who Jesus was for the better part of his life on earth. At least three things are noteworthy about Jesus as carpenter.

First, Jesus experienced what we would call a blue-collar life. He could relate to the majority of first-century folk in Nazareth. He knew what it was like to "punch a clock," to pull splinters from his palms and nurse scabs that turned to calluses. He understood the daily grind of manual labor, the exchange of goods and services with customers, and the important balance of quality and efficiency.

Have you ever imagined a table built by Jesus? How beautiful it would be, how precise its dimensions, and how perfect its function. How many flaws would you expect to find? The question sounds almost absurd, doesn't it? This is precisely the line of thinking taken by Dorothy Sayers in her essay "Why Work?," quoted above, where she considers what the Christian religion has to say about our work. She writes:

> But is it astonishing? How can any one remain interested in a religion which seems to have no concern with nine-tenths of his life? The Church's approach to an intelligent carpenter is usually confined to exhorting him not to be drunk and disorderly in his leisure hours, and to come to church on Sundays. What the Church *should* be telling him is this: that the very first demand that his religion makes upon him is that he should make good tables.
>
> Church by all means, and decent forms of amusement, certainly—but what use is all that if in the very center of his life and occupation he is insulting God with bad carpentry? No crooked table legs or ill-fitting drawers ever, I dare swear, came out of the carpenter's shop at Nazareth. Nor, if they did, could anyone believe that they were made by the same hand that made Heaven and earth. No piety in the worker will compensate for work that is not true to itself; for any work that is untrue to its own technique is a living lie.[3]

Sayers' words are haunting for Christian workers today. Whether carpenter, cab driver, or candlestick maker, we must *work true:* Our work agrees with the truth that the kingdom of heaven has come to earth and God is at work through his people making all things new—even in our table-making.

Second, Jesus came in flesh and blood, just like us. This may seem far too obvious, but it is important to mention since many Christians live as though the only important dimension of reality is the spiritual dimension. To be sure, the Bible teaches that there is a spiritual side of God's world—the spirit of human beings, for example—but nowhere does the Bible teach that the spiritual dimension is superior to the material dimension. Instead, the two are necessary and equal parts of creation that have different functions. Indeed, the bodily birth, life, death, and resurrection of Jesus (not to mention his carpentry profession) testify to the significance of the material world in proper relationship with the spiritual.

In light of this, Christians should be careful of prioritizing the spiritual over the physical. This often happens, for example, in our missions efforts. When we end with evangelism, rather than beginning with it, we assume that securing the soul's salvation is all that matters instead of recognizing that salvation is the beginning of a person's walk with the Savior who "became flesh and dwelt among us" (John 1:14). Further, when we reduce the Christian disciplines to "spiritual" disciplines, we neglect the opportunity—indeed, the responsibility—to keep and cultivate the garden that is God's world. When we neglect the material realm, we reinforce the lie that this aspect of God's creation is no longer good and perhaps no longer his at all. I suspect that the "meek" who "shall inherit the earth" (Matt 5:5) would beg to differ.

Third, work and workers were often on Jesus' mind, and they held a central place in his teaching—especially his parables. His "blue-collar" experience set him on common ground with the people rather than on a perch of privilege from which to talk down to them like the religious leaders did. Of course, even some of the commoners resisted Jesus' teaching and authority. As he said, it's hard to be a prophet in one's hometown. Nonetheless, workers and their work were never far from Jesus' mind and thus never far from his teaching.

Work in the Gospels and Acts

The word *ergon* (and its linguistic family) is the dominant Greek term translated as "work" in English New Testaments. It occurs more than 200 times and can be translated in various ways, including "work," "task," "engaging in activity," "industrial work" (such as farming, tilling, weaving), and "the final product of work."

Ergon also refers to works of good versus works of evil, connecting to our discussion of "work" and "works" above. For example, in Matthew 23:2–4, Jesus condemns the scribes and Pharisees for the "works they do," which burden the people (although they don't practice what they preach). Further, in Luke 13:27, Jesus says, "Then you will begin to say, 'We ate and drank in your presence, and you taught in our streets.' But he will say, 'I tell you, I do not know where you come from. Depart from me, all you workers of evil!"

Of Jesus' more than 40 parables in the Gospels, at least 20 pertain to workers and their work, including:

- The parable of the Sower (Matt 13:1–9)

- The parable of the Talents (Matt 25:14–30)

- The parable of the Prodigal Son (Luke 15:11–32)

- The laborers in the vineyard (Matt 20:1–16)

- The two builders (Matt 7:24–27)

- The waiting servants (Luke 12:35–48)

If workers and work comprise nearly 50 percent of Jesus' parables, what effect should this have on the church's teaching and preaching today? Not surprisingly, this theme extends beyond Jesus' parables and hold an important role in his didactic instruction as well. We'll survey Jesus' teaching in John 4-6 and 17 and his parable of the waiting servants from Luke 12:35-48, focusing on workers and work.

John 4-6 & 17 — God's Work

The first mention of work in this gospel appears in John 4:34, after Jesus' disciples urged him to eat. He replied, "My food is to do the will of him who sent me and to accomplish his work [*ergon*]." Following two more healing scenes — the Capernaum official's son and the invalid at the pool of Bethesda — Jesus continues this theme by stating, "My

Father is working until now, and I am working" (5:17). John 6 opens with Jesus feeding the 5,000, followed by his miraculous walking on water. Beginning in 6:22, then, John reminds us of the intertwined nature of food and work and directs us to the reality that Jesus is the bread of life. Jesus replies in 6:26–35:

> "Truly, truly, I say to you, you are seeking me, not because you saw signs, but because you ate your fill of the loaves. Do not work for the food that perishes, but for the food that endures to eternal life, which the Son of Man will give to you. For on him God the Father has set his seal." Then they said to him, "What must we do, to be doing the works of God?" Jesus answered them, "This is the work of God, that you believe in him whom he has sent. ... Truly, truly, I say to you, it was not Moses who gave you the bread from heaven, but my Father gives you the true bread from heaven. For the bread of God is he who comes down from heaven and gives life to the world." They said to him, "Sir, give us this bread always." Jesus said to them, "I am the bread of life; whoever comes to shall not hunger, and whoever believes in me shall never thirst."

In keeping with his own words from 4:34, Jesus first instructs his followers not to work for perishable food but for the food that brings eternal life. After the disciples seek clarity about how they can do the "works of God," Jesus insists that the work of God is faith in the Son (6:29). Finally, Jesus reveals the strong link between work, faith, and food: He is the bread of life. Not only this, but his work as the bread of life that came down from heaven gives life to the world.

The deep and mysterious connection between work, faith, and food from John 6 has occupied theologians for centuries. Our purpose here is not to untangle the knot of John 6, important as it is, but rather to note the important parallel between Jesus' work and our work.

Could it be that our work—work wrapped around faith in Jesus, the Son sent by God—joins with God's work in giving life to the world? In this passage, we detect three tasks for believers to do: (1) work for eternal, not temporal, food; (2) work in faith that Jesus is the Son sent from God; (3) let the reward of our work be feasting on Christ, who is the Bread of Life. By partaking of the true food and true drink that comes from faith-filled work, we are given eternal life (6:53–56).

So do we, in fact, join Jesus in giving life to the world? Jesus' prayer in John 17 helps answer this question. Jesus returns to the theme of work in 17:4–5: "I glorified you on earth, having accomplished the work you gave me to do. And now, Father, glorify me in your own presence with the glory that I had with you before the world existed." Then, in 17:6, Jesus turns his attention to the people who believe in and follow God. In the beautiful verses that follow, Jesus' prayer commissions his followers to continue his work in the world. He prays specifically for two kinds of protection. He doesn't pray for the physical safety of his people as we might expect; in fact, Jesus is clear that the world already hates them just as they hated him (17:14). Instead, Jesus prays for protection from the evil one and for unity among the people. He says, "Holy Father, keep them in your name, which you have given me, that they may be one, even as we are one" (17:11).

John 17:20-21 finalizes our point. Here, Jesus effectively hands off the work of God to his followers—those given, to him by the Father—through his prayer:

> I do not ask for these only, but also for those who believe in me through their word, that they may all be one, just as you, Father, are in me, and I in you, that they also may be in us, so that they world may believe that you have sent me.

Now, with the help of the Holy Spirit promised in John 16:7, those who believe in the Son—those who labor for eternal food and feast on the true food and drink—join Jesus in giving life to the world. Jesus is life itself. As such, the degree to which we wrap our physical and spiritual work around faith in the Son, feast on his true flesh and blood, and exercise a united love for God and neighbor is the degree to which we, the lights of the world, give life to the world.

Luke 12:35-48—Kingdom Faithfulness, Stewardship, and Responsibility

The parable of the waiting servants centers on three characters and two main themes. The characters include the master of the household (Jesus), the manager of the household, and the servants. The parable revolves around the themes of readiness and blessedness. Further, it is broken into two parts interrupted by Peter's question concerning to whom the parable is addressed.

In part one, Jesus begins with the imperative "Be ready!"[4] By this he means readiness for the master's return: "Blessed are those servants whom the master finds awake when he comes" (12:37). The master could return at any time, day or night—thus, be *ready!* This is Jesus' first hint in Luke's Gospel at his approaching departure and return. He wants his disciples to feel the weight of kingdom responsibility— the very thing for which he urged them to seek and sell everything just a few verses earlier. Thus, the thrust of part one to be on guard—those who are *ready* will be *blessed.*[5]

Peter interjects in Luke 12:41: "Lord, are You telling this parable for us or for all?" Jesus replies with part two of the parable, offering greater detail and further character development. The rest of the parable takes place between the faithful manager, who is rewarded for his wise stewardship, and the foolish manager, who is severely punished for his dereliction and misconduct. The differences between the two are primarily seen in the way they run their respective households, but Jesus appears to be more concerned with the motivation for their actions.

Beginning in 12:45, Jesus says:

> But if that servant says to himself, "My master is delaying his coming," and begins to beat the

> male and female servants, and to eat and drink
> and get drunk, the master of that servant will
> come on a day when he does not expect him and
> at an hour he does not know, and will cut him
> in pieces and put him with the unfaithful (Luke
> 12:45–46).

Jesus uses the term "servant" here even though he is still referring to the manager. Perhaps this is a subtle hint for managers not to think too highly of themselves. Nonetheless, Jesus begins by acknowledging the manager's poor assumption that the master of the household "is delayed in coming." Assuming there's no urgency, the foolish manager abuses his authority by beating his workers and stealing food from the estate, only to be surprised by the master's return. This manager, now downgraded to slave, is *cut into pieces* and counted as an unbeliever.

The faithful manager, however, stewards his master's household with wisdom and care.[6] He feeds his employees on time and remains diligent in all his duties—and he was not caught off guard when the master returned. When the master returned to find a working manager and well-ordered household, he rewarded the wise manager and "set him over all his possessions" (12:44).

From a Christian perspective on work, we must consider two applications from this passage. First, notice the emphasis on full-time faithfulness and wise stewardship. In this parable, Jesus' praise is not primarily about skill and quality of work, but about faithfulness and wisdom. Regardless of whether we identify more with manager or the servant, the master expects all of us to be faithful and wise in our responsibilities such that we are neither caught off guard nor ashamed of our work when he returns.

Second, we see that everything we have belongs to the master. This includes what we have at work. Paul reminds us of this in 1 Corinthians 4:7 when he asks, "What do you have that you did not receive?" These gifts include both material and immaterial things. For example, my desk, computer, books, and coffee mug—all essential tools for my vocation (especially the coffee mug)—belong to the Master. Further, my time, energy, relationships with colleagues, and spiritual gifts also belong to the Master. Both tangible, material things and intangible, invisible things belong to the Master, and he has entrusted them to me expecting that I will steward them wisely and faithfully.

Abraham Kuyper is right when he says, "There is not a square inch in the whole domain of our human existence over which Christ ... does not cry, 'Mine!' "[7] Kuyper's words alert us to Christ's sovereignty over the whole of creation, although we often don't allow this truth to reach into the immaterial areas of our lives, such as our time and energies. Perhaps, then, we could stretch it further to suggest that there is not a waking (or resting!) hour in my entire calendar where Christ hasn't called a meeting.

The ultimate question here is what you are doing with the Master's possessions. Consider how you manage the time, talents, possessions, and places he has given you, especially at work. Are you faithfully and wisely attending to these things? Or are you negligent, jealous of others, and lazy? Are you treating employees and colleagues with the dignity and respect they deserve as image-bearers, or do you abuse your authority, talk badly about your boss, and steal time and resources from the company?

Consider what double love of God and neighbor looks like for your job. The Master is eager to bless the faithful, but those he finds unfaithful must beware, for to whom much is given, much is required (Luke 12:48).

Work in the Letters and Revelation

The theme of work remains prominent throughout the New Testament letters and the book of Revelation. Particularly in Paul's letters, it's important to keep in mind the distinction between work and works (as previously discussed). For Paul, the wrong kind of work is that which attempts to earn God's favor. The right kind of work is the fruit of faith, which manifests itself in both spiritual and material ways, loving God and others in word *and* deed.

To understand Paul's view of work, it's important that we look to 2 Timothy 3:16–17. Here, he writes, "All Scripture is breathed out by God and profitable for teaching, for reproof, for correction, and for training in righteousness, that the man [or woman] of God may be complete, equipped for every good work" [*ergon*].

Paul is not suggesting here that the Bible is the instruction manual for every kind of labor. Indeed, it isn't much help when it comes to diesel mechanics. It is, however, God's Word to us about who he is and about how his world works.

Further, the Scriptures tell us who we are and how we ought to live in God's world. Thus, while it isn't a how-to manual for mechanics, it is profitable for Christian autoworkers who seek to do their work in a way that proclaims the kingdom of God is here. The way of righteousness to which Christians are called extends to the quality of our work, the timeliness of our work, our treatment of customers, how we handle money, and much more. The same is true for every vocation in the kingdom.

Paul insists that our union with Christ results in newness of life and, therefore, a new *way* of life that affects even our work—hence Paul's emphasis on good works in Ephesians 2:10. For Paul, then, there is no place for laziness, as in the case with the Thessalonians. Instead, our work of faith should be a "labor of love" (1 Thess 1:3), leading a quiet life, minding our own business, and working with our hands (1 Thess 4:11). We embody Paul's command to "walk in a manner worthy" of our calling in Christ (Col 1:10) by *working* worthy of our calling with all love, wisdom, and understanding (see Col 4; Eph 4–5; 1 Thess 2). To do so, our work must be fueled by our love for God, which then spills over into love for God's world.

The author of Hebrews reminds us that our working God created all things through his Son, the one who "is the radiance of the glory of God and the exact imprint of his nature, and he upholds the universe by the word of his power" (Heb 1:3). Further, this Son is the heir of all things and the one "through whom he created the world" (Heb 1:2). After believing in and being united to this Son, then, we join the family of God and are motivated to "stir up one another to love and good *works*" (Heb 10:24).

James joins the chorus, adding further clarity concerning the relationship between faith and work/works. In James 2:18, he argues, "But someone will say, 'You have faith and I have works.' Show me your faith apart from your works, and I will show you my faith by my works." At first glance, one might conclude that James and Paul are at odds, but rest assured, they are not. Instead, James and Paul both are aiming at the same target but from different angles. Paul's emphasis begins with faith and then moves to works; James emphasizes the importance of works as fruit in a Christian's life, since such fruit is the evidence of faith. James does not undermine the faith-then-works position; rather, as a rightly irritated early church leader, his rhetoric calls for more walk and less talk from his flock.

In his second letter, Peter writes, "But the day of the Lord will come like a thief, and then the heavens will pass away with a roar, and the heavenly bodies will be burned up and dissolved, and the earth and the works that are done on it will be exposed" (2 Pet 3:10). It is difficult to understate the effect this one verse has had on Christians of the last century. Many have interpreted this verse to mean that on the Day of the Lord, all of creation will be annihilated and created brand new, *ex nihilo*, all over again. We seek to offer another view.

To begin, we must remember that everything God created was "very good" (Gen 1:31). Everything that exists—seen and unseen—was created by God through Christ (John 1:1–3;

Heb 1:1–3), and everything that was created by our good God is intrinsically good. That's great news! The bad news is that sin has wreaked havoc on God's good world. But what God made good, sin cannot make bad. Instead, sin acts as a parasite, defiling God's good work for unrighteous ends. Sin is not capable of creating something new the way God has done. It can only corrupt what already exists. The rest of Scripture teaches that God is at work making all things new through Jesus and his *work* on earth—namely, his death and resurrection. Now, when we unite with Christ and are filled with God's Spirit, we are empowered with "the ministry of reconciliation" (2 Cor 5:18) to proclaim the gospel and with works worthy of our calling in Christ.

How does this affect our reading of 2 Peter 3:10? First, we must keep the whole Bible in mind when reading Scripture. In so doing, we maintain a clearer view of creation as God's good work, which he has not forsaken. Second, we must allow other passages of Scripture to inform our understanding. For example, 1 Corinthians 3:9 teaches that "we are God's fellow workers" as well as "God's building." After explaining that God has built on the foundation of Christ, Paul argues:

> If anyone builds on the foundation with gold, silver, precious stones, wood, hay, straw—each one's work will become manifest, for the Day will disclose it, because it will be revealed by fire, and the fire will test what sort of work each one has done. If the work that anyone has built on the foundation survives, he will receive a

reward. If anyone's work is burned up, he will suffer loss, though he himself will be saved, but only as through fire (1 Cor 3:12–15).

Although both 2 Peter 3 and 1 Corinthians 3 carry their own ambiguities, we can conclude a few things. First, the language of both appears to state that "through fire" all of creation will be *disclosed*, not destroyed. In other words, we should expect a purging or refining of creation rather than annihilation. Second, this disclosing is similar to what happened in the flood of Genesis 7–8, though this time sin will not squeak through as it did before. Because of Christ, sin will be snuffed out and death destroyed in the new heavens and earth. Third, we can infer that our work will be seen on the other side. Paul's language is often read as speaking only to the fruit of our spiritual work, but perhaps the fruit of our physical work will greet us in the kingdom as well.[8]

A scholar friend of mine once remarked, "When we reach the new heavens and new earth, one of the first things I'll do is dash off to the library." When I asked him why, he replied in his cheeky way, "To see if my books made it through." His point is not an egotistical one. Rather, he longs for his works to be of such value—gold, silver, and precious stone—that they might have a place in Christ's eternal kingdom.

One wonders if this is what Revelation 21:24–26 refers to: "By its light [the glory of God] will the nations walk, and the kings of the earth will bring their glory into it. ... They will bring into it the glory and the honor of the nations." We don't know for certain what the "glory and honor of the nations" are, but we can't help but wonder, what glory do the nations have to offer in the light of the glory of God? Could the glory of the nations be good works done in faith? If so, would these be strictly spiritual works, or also physical works?

We cannot answer these questions with certainty, but we believe we can there will be some continuity between this world and the one to come. Will it be new? Of course; otherwise it could not be the *new* heavens and earth. But some things will be old, beginning with the Ancient of Days himself.

Conclusion

Our first concluding reflection highlights that nowhere does the New Testament relegate work to a lower class. Instead, work is basic to being human. Hierarchical cultures relegate manual labor to the lower classes and privilege the higher classes, who fill their bellies from the labor of others. The Christian view of work turns this on its head. As Paul insists, "If anyone is not willing to work, let him not eat" (2 Thess 3:10).

Second, we recognize the Trinitarian nature of work in the New Testament. John 4–6 and Ephesians 1–2 especially underscore the integral role of Father, Son, and Spirit in all of the work of God. In creation, salvation, new creation, and beyond, it is only through the work of the Son and the empowering of the Spirit that all things will ultimately be restored to the glory of God the Father.

Finally, we recognize a mysterious but critical relationship between faith and work/works. We argued for a "faith, then works" view with respect to our salvation, and that both are fundamental to our relationship with Christ at the moment we are reborn as well as in day-to-day life. The effect of our faith does not end with regeneration. Rather, our faith remains at the center of our union with Christ. Thus we wrap our work around faith in Jesus and join him in giving life to the world.

Action Points

- How does your work relate to God's work in John 6; 17?

- How can you manage your calendar differently to reflect obedience to Christ?

- How does the reality of heaven affect the way you approach menial tasks at work?

Recommended Reading

Bauckham, Richard. *Bible and Mission: Christian Witness in a Postmodern World*. Grand Rapids: Baker Academic, 2003.

Bratt, James D., ed. *Abraham Kuyper: A Centennial Reader*. Grand Rapids: Eerdmans, 1998.

Stevens, R. Paul. *Work Matters: Lessons from Scripture*. Grand Rapids: Eerdmans, 2012.

Stevens, R. Paul. *The Other Six Days: Vocation, Work, and Ministry in Biblical Perspective*. Grand Rapids: Eerdmans, 2000.

CHAPTER 4

Christ, Wisdom, and Work

O wisdom, the sweetest light of a purified mind! Woe to those who abandon you as their guide and ramble about where you have left your traces, who love the things in which you speak to us instead of loving you, and forget what you are telling us. For you do not cease to tell us what and how great you are, and you speak to us in the beauty of every created thing. Even a craftsman somehow speaks in the very beauty of his work to the one who sees it, bidding him not to devote all his attention to the appearance of the material object that has been produced, but to look beyond it and recall with affection the one who produced it. But those who love what you make instead of loving you are like people who hear someone speaking wisely and eloquently and listen keenly to the charm of his voice and the construction of his words, while ignoring the most important thing: the meaning that his words signified.[1]

—ST. AUGUSTINE, *De libero arbitrio*

As a teenager, my dad often reminded my older brother and me (Benjamin), "Be wise men; make wise decisions." On several occasions I remember thinking, "On the one hand, I know exactly what he means—don't be stupid. On the other hand, I can't define wisdom or provide a set of criteria for wise versus unwise decisions."

Despite my teenage limitations, I noticed that people in general—and Christians in particular—are keen on the notion of wisdom, and most would admit their desire to live accordingly. But what is wisdom and how does it relate to our lives, especially our work?

Christ and Wisdom

Two truths provide the foundation for a Christian view of wisdom. First is the reality that Jesus is "the wisdom of God" (1 Cor 1:24). Second is that wisdom created the world (Prov 3:19–20; 8:22–36; Jer 10:12; 51:15). In light of this, we understand that the creator of the world is Jesus, the eternal Son, Word of God, and wisdom incarnate.[2] But what does it matter that the "wisdom of God" made the world? How does that affect our view of creation and the way we ought to live in God's world?

We begin by acknowledging that this is God's world. With the psalmist we declare:

> The earth is the LORD's and the fullness thereof,
>   the world and those who dwell therein,
> for he has founded it upon the seas
>   and established it upon the rivers (Psa 24:1–2).

What God made good, sin did not make bad, nor has it stolen what God made away from him. Instead, creation still belongs to God, and we, as God's image-bearers, are still responsible for stewarding his world according to his ways. As the psalmist further declares:

> May you be blessed by the LORD,
>   who made heaven and earth.
>
> The heavens are the LORD's heavens,
>   but the earth he has given to the children of
>   man (Psa 115:15–16).

Thus, we begin with the declaration that God is king of creation, his creation is good, and we are responsible for being wise stewards.[3]

Moreover, we acknowledge the significance of wisdom incarnate serving as the craftsman of creation (Prov 8:30). In the epigraph to this chapter, we quote St. Augustine referencing the traces of wisdom in what has been made. He writes, "For you do not cease to tell us what and how great you are, and you speak to us in the beauty of every created thing."[4] Indeed, just as a woodworker leaves his mark on what he has made, so Christ has left traces of himself on all that He created.

Wisdom in (Not "of") the World

Creation was built by wisdom, and thus wisdom was built into creation. Through Christ, God created the world in a particular way. By means of his Word, God created things that can be tasted, touched, smelled, heard, and seen; other created things cannot be sensed at all but are nevertheless real. The human soul, for example, is as real as the body, according to Scripture, but it can't be dissected or placed under a microscope. God created a variety of species—including humans, sheep, oxen, birds of the sky, fish of the sea, insects, and creeping things—all of which declare his magnificence (Psa 8:1–9). He created earthy stuff, watery stuff, and cloudy stuff, all full of texture and color. He also built potential into his creation that can be developed in incredible ways. Art, culture, music, politics, architecture, language, economics, technology, medicine—each of these unfold as people work with the potential God placed in the world. This is the *imago dei* (image of God) at work in human beings.

God's wisdom, along with his other attributes, makes all of this possible. He has both the knowledge and ability to create, and he is powerful enough to create *ex nihilo*—out of nothing. Nothing else is capable of creating out of nothing. We can develop and manipulate creation, but we can't make something out of nothing. We can only tinker with the toys that already exist.

This illustrates the important divide between the Creator and creation. God is not like us. He does not depend on other things for his existence. We, however, need many things—food, water, oxygen, and a beating heart, just to name a few—all of which come from God. In his wisdom, he has built a world that by its very nature points to a great provider, and in his love and grace he provides what we need.

God's wisdom is also made known in the world through order, limits, and laws. Although creation sometimes exhibits erratic behavior, causing great damage and disorder through natural disasters, diseases, etc., this is not what God intended. Scripture suggests that in the beginning, God's world operated according to the order he built into it. Animals were at peace with one another. Humans managed God's world with wisdom and love without frustration or toil. *Shalom* was the song of the cosmos, and God walked in the garden with his creatures.

In addition to order, God also created laws and limits in the beginning, establishing the proper ways, direction, and boundaries of creation. We observe the laws of nature when gravity holds our feet on the ground or when we see how the planets orbit. God enacts these laws directly, as only he can. Laws pertaining to morality (we might call these moral norms) are etched into the order of creation, but they are entrusted to us to be maintained.[5]

The limits of creation, then, are seen both in the material sense and the immaterial sense. In Job 38:8–11, for example, God asks Job:

> Who shut in the sea with doors
>   when it burst out from the womb,
> when I made clouds its garment
>   and thick darkness its swaddling band,
> and prescribed limits for it
>   and set bars and doors,
>   and said, "Thus far shall you come, and no
>   farther,
> and here shall your proud waves be stayed"?

In this passage we recognize God's authority over creation as well as the limits he has established. Invisible limits often fall particularly into the moral dimension of creation. Ray Van Leeuwen writes, "Love of Wisdom means staying within her prescribed cosmic-social boundaries; love of Folly, like love of another's wife, means simply the deadly pursuit of things out of bounds ... Thus, recognition of cosmic structure or limits is inseparable from proper *eros* or direction."[6] In other words, just as God's world was created in a particular way with order, laws, and limits, there is also a certain way in which people ought to live in God's world.

Wisdom's Way

The theme of "way" is prevalent throughout the Bible, especially in Wisdom literature. Proverbs, in particular, is aptly summarized as the book of two ways: One is the way of wisdom, and the other is the way of folly—there is no middle ground. Proverbs is a father's exhortation to his children to forsake the way of folly, which ends in death, and walk instead in the way of wisdom. But if we are expected to follow a particular way, where do we begin, where do we end, and how do we get started? These three—beginning, end, and way—are integral parts to any journey.

Starting Place

Scripture is unabashed about the proper starting place for life. Proverbs 1:7 declares, "The fear of the Lord is the beginning of knowledge; fools despise wisdom and instruction."[7]

Further, Proverbs 9:10 adds, "The fear of the LORD is the beginning of wisdom, and the knowledge of the Holy One is insight."

The importance of the fear of the Lord as the proper beginning for the human journey can hardly be overemphasized. The entire history of Israel can be understood in terms of periods when they feared the Lord and followed his way versus times when they refused to fear him and followed their own way. Moses summed up God's requirement of his people by saying, "And now, Israel, what does the LORD your God require of you, but to fear the LORD your God, to walk in all his ways, to love him, to serve the LORD your God with all your heart and with all your soul" (Deut 10:12). More often than not, however, the Israelites stiffened their necks and walked their own way. As Isaiah described, "Was it not the LORD, against whom we have sinned, in whose ways they would not walk, and whose law they would not obey?" (Isa 42:24).[8]

The "fear of the Lord" also includes three critical ingredients to human flourishing. The first is a healthy understanding of "fear." I often hear the question, "Does 'fear of the Lord' literally mean to be afraid or scared of God?" To this I answer yes, although that isn't all that is meant by "fear" as used in these verses. The Hebrew word for fear (*yirah*) implies terror, reverence, and piety. Thus, it is right for people to be frightened of God when they live in opposition to his ways. In more positive terms, however, the "fear of the Lord" nurtures reverence and worship in those who walk in the way of the Lord, leading to deeper love and a fuller life with God.

Second, "fear of the Lord" insists on fear and faith in a particular God—Yahweh, the God of Abraham, Isaac, and Jacob. This God declares himself as the one true God, wholly set apart from anything in creation and not to be confused with the gods of other nations.[9]

Third, "fear of the Lord" requires spiritual and intellectual humility. Fear of the Lord serves as the threshold to the way of wisdom. In that sense, it is equivalent to humility—the first step on that path. It is impossible for anyone to cross the "fear of the Lord" threshold and hold onto intellectual elitism or swollen pride. Human heads, hearts, and achievements simply will not fit through the door without a proper cleansing by the one who declared, "I am the door" and "I am the way."[10]

Ending Place (Telos)

What is the *telos* ("end" or "goal") of the Christian life? Scripture is clear about "fear of the Lord" as the starting place for the way of wisdom, but where do we end? What are we aiming at?

The Christian *telos* is multifaceted. First, the aim of Christian living is the Great Commandment. Jesus said the most important thing about living in God's world is to love God and love neighbor.[11] Jesus speaks of these two commandments as almost one in the same, for when we properly love God, we will inevitably love others. Further, this twofold commandment underscores the importance of balancing the vertical and horizontal dimensions of life. Some tend to focus their love and efforts inordinately on the vertical dimension, running the risk of being so heavenly minded that they're no earthly good. Others focus too much on the horizontal dimension, busying themselves with good works but neglecting God and the gospel along the way. The twin commandments of loving God and loving neighbor demand a "both/and" orientation, not an "either/or." Our love begins with God, then spills over into love toward his world—and this order must never be reversed! Indeed, as our love for God grows, it will increasingly resemble the love that the Father has for his world.[12]

Secondly, the Christian *telos* is Christlikeness. In Ephesians 4:1-16, for example, Paul's primary goal is to call Christians to maturity by "[walking] in a manner worthy of the calling to which you have been called." The "walking" language alerts us to the way of wisdom we see in the Old Testament, yet it also points us to the goal of the way, which is Christlike maturity. This kind of maturity is characterized by humility, gentleness, patience, and love, all of which are the result of God's Spirit at work in people (Eph 4:1-3). Christ is our head and our aim. He is the "end (*telos*) of the law of righteousness" and the exemplar for every person.[13]

The Way In Between

Knowing where to begin and where to end is vital for anyone on a journey, since these two points provide proper direction for the trip. The bulk of time, however, is spent on the way in between these two points. So, what is the way? This is less a directional question and more an inquiry into wise living in between the proper beginning and ending points.

We begin by recalling the rich theme of "way" throughout Scripture as noted above. In the New Testament we are especially reminded of Jesus' reference to himself as "the way" in John 14:6, the reference to the first Christians being called followers of "the Way" in Acts 9:2, and Paul's frequent metaphor of "walking" to illustrate the Christian life.

To understand the way of wisdom, then, we need look no further than the wise woman of Proverbs 31:10-31. We summarized this passage in chapter 2, so we will be brief here. Wisdom is personified as a woman throughout the Bible, especially in Wisdom literature. Proverbs 31 zooms in to provide a picture of the day-to-day life of Lady Wisdom. Here are few things to note about her:

1. She fears the Lord (31:30).

2. She is fully human—both material and spiritual matters are of highest concern for her (31:10-31).

3. She is trustworthy (31:11).

4. She speaks with wisdom (31:26).

5. She does good, not evil, at all times (31:12).

6. She willingly works with her hands (31:13).

7. She cares for her house by rising early, tending to clothes and linens, working in the field, and feeding the family (31:13-22).

8. She cares for the poor (31:20).

9. She invests and earns profit (31:16, 24).

We could list more characteristics, but these highlight what the author of Proverbs wants readers to notice about wise living. The Proverbs 31 woman walks—that is, she lives, works, talks, sells, invests, etc.—the *right* way. She begins by fearing the Lord, then she lives. Wise living for her is not reduced merely to spiritual matters, nor is she guilty of Martha's folly of busyness. This wise woman understands the "way" in between God-fearing and Christlikeness to be full of (1) a focus on others, (2) maintaining goodness, justice, and loving-kindness, and (3) the cultivation of creation.

We can easily see how the life of the wise woman is focused on others. One might argue that her entire life is wrapped up in doing for others. Her service is not limited to her immediate family; she serves her entire household, which includes her husband and children as well as her servants. Yes, the wise woman serves the servants (31:15). Further, she anticipates cold weather and ensures that her household is doubly clothed (31:21). She's never idle (31:27); as a result, she's rewarded for her labor, and "her works praise her in the gates" (31:31).

Moreover, the Proverbs 31 woman's character is built on goodness, justice, and loving-kindness. "She does [her husband] good, and not harm, all the days of her life" (31:12). And again, we see that her service reaches beyond her household. Just as she "puts her hands" to the spinning, she also extends her hands to the poor and needy (31:19–20).

She neither judges their station in life nor separates herself from their condition. She does justly, loves mercy, and walks humbly with her God as she reaches out to those who have need. [14] And when she speaks, her words are not lofty and elitist, but soft-spoken and gentle. When she opens her mouth, people perk up to listen, for "wisdom, and the teaching of kindness is on her tongue" (31:26).[15]

Finally, the wise woman cultivates creation and contributes to the broader society as an investor, gardener, and entrepreneur. The passage speaks of her buying a field and then planting a garden. She puts her sewing skills to work by designing linen garments and belts, which she then sells to local merchants. The wise woman is resourceful both in terms of skills and finances. Nowhere, however, do we sense that the reason for her investment is to make herself rich. Instead, she invests her profits to benefit others. To be sure, the Proverbs 31 woman doesn't shy away from profit. She's aware of cost versus benefit, and she considers the return on her investment. The difference, however, is the end to which she invests, gardens, and sells. Her goal is not more for herself, but flourishing for all.

Wisdom at Work

The way of wisdom is the link between wisdom and work. This way finds its beginning in the fear of the Lord and finds its *telos* in the love of God and neighbor and in Christlike maturity. The wise woman models the way in between by providing a picture of well-ordered vocation. She demonstrates wisdom in all of her callings—mother, neighbor, entrepreneur, spouse—though here we especially have in mind the place of employment.

The economy of the home that we see in Proverbs 31 is a microcosm of God's economy of all things. When we zoom out and consider the whole of God's world, we can ask what Proverbs 31 would look like if the wise woman were a mechanic, librarian, truck driver, artist ... fill in the blank with your job, and imagine how the passage would apply to your life.

Many Christians today find it difficult to overcome the dualism that prioritizes spiritual matters over material matters, and it hinders our ability to appreciate our jobs. We believe, however, that secularism is a lie. If it's true that God created all things and declared them "very good" (Gen 1:31), and if it's true that "the earth is the LORD's and the fullness thereof, the world and those who dwell therein" (Psa 24:1), then everything is sacred. Sin may corrupt and misdirect God's good world toward bad ends, but it cannot make bad what God made good.

Instead, God is at work making all things new, and he has given his people the privilege of joining with him in the process. We do this by first embracing our ministries. God has given us the "ministry of reconciliation," a topic Paul addresses in 2 Corinthians 5:18. After reconciling us to himself through Christ, God bestows this ministry on his people for us to apply the healing power of the gospel to the brokenness in his world.

So, does this ministry focus on evangelism and discipleship, or is it a ministry of good deeds and acts of love and mercy? Yes! Once again, this is not an "either/or," but a "both/and." The reconciling power of the gospel addresses spiritual, physical, structural, mental, relational, and every other kind of brokenness. We must never minimize the importance of verbally sharing the good news of Jesus' life, death, burial, and resurrection and calling people to repentance and faith. And we must not be found handing gospel tracts to hungry people without feeding them.

Conclusion

After embracing our ministry of reconciliation, we must get to work—especially at work! Every job is different, and thus applying wisdom and reconciliation at work will look different for each of us. Therefore, it is best to avoid offering a one-size-fits-all approach and instead suggest a series of questions to consider.

Consider how your responsibilities at work relate to and serve God's world. For example, truck drivers don't simply move boxes from point A to point B. They feed families by delivering food to the local markets and grocery stores. Without truck drivers, the economy would suffer greatly, and many families would struggle to find food. Further, consider all the people truck drivers come into contact with. Every relationship brings an opportunity to love our neighbor. We cannot underestimate the meaningfulness of genuine, thoughtful interaction with other people. The effect that a doubly-loving truck driver can have on others is immeasurable.

Consider whether you can work in a way that better respects the Creator, the dignity of other people (including yourself), or the goodness of creation. Insofar as you're able, how can you redirect your tasks and responsibilities toward love of God and neighbor? If you're not able to make these changes, how can you advocate for a better way?

Finally, ask yourself, "How does my 'ministry' of work contribute to God's mission of making all things new?" For an artist, for instance, this question may be easy to answer. For the factory worker, it may be more difficult. Nevertheless, when we connect our jobs—no matter their nature—to God's economy of all things, we better understand the meaningfulness of the work of our hands. God takes our meager loaves and fishes and multiplies them to give life to the world.

Action Points

- What is wisdom, and how does one become wise?

- Where does wisdom begin? Where is its end?

- How are the "ways" of your work out of rhythm with the "way of wisdom"? To answer this question, consider additional questions such as whether there is a better way to lead your team at work, coach your kids, instruct in the classroom, deliver the mail, invest your money, work the field, build houses, etc.

Recommended Reading

Augustine. *The Confessions.* Trans. R. S. Pine-Coffin. New York: Penguin Books, 1961.

Bartholomew, Craig G., and Ryan P. O'Dowd. *Old Testament Wisdom Literature: A Theological Introduction.* Downers Grove, IL: IVP Academic, 2011.

Kuyper, Abraham. *Wisdom and Wonder: Common Grace in Science and Art.* Ed. Jordan J. Ballor and Stephen J. Grabill. Trans. Nelson D. Kloosterman. Bellingham, WA: Lexham Press, 2015.

Van Leeuwen, Raymond. "Proverbs." In *The New Interpreter's Bible: Proverbs–Sirach*, Vol. 5. Nashville: Abingdon Press, 1997.

Wolters, Albert M. *Creation Regained: Biblical Basics for a Reformational Worldview.* Grand Rapids: Eerdmans, 2005.

Wolters, Albert M. *The Song of the Valiant Woman.* Bletchley, UK: Paternoster Press, 2001.

Wright, N. T. *After You Believe: Why Christian Character Matters.* New York: HarperOne, 2012.

CHAPTER 5

Putting It All Together: Kingdom, Mission, and Discipleship

> *More often ... [workers] are simply instructed to be people of strong integrity and to seek to win coworkers for Christ. These emphases on ethics and evangelism are needed and valuable, but they are insufficient for equipping Christians to steward their vocational power to advance foretastes of the kingdom. We need to get beyond the status quo.*[1]
>
> —AMY L. SHERMAN, *Kingdom Calling*

The kingdom is the objective of God's mission, and it stands as the referent for our work as we seek to manifest the kingdom. The notion of the kingdom has always been difficult for me to grasp. If the kingdom is a confusing concept for you, don't worry; you are in good company. Renowned

New Testament scholar I. Howard Marshall admits that although the kingdom of God has been the subject of a great deal of biblical research in recent years, its meaning is not often clear.[2]

Kingdom and Work

Stephen J. Nichols helps us understand that the all-encompassing nature of God's kingdom makes the concept very difficult to conceptualize. The kingdom has implications for every part of theology and God's mission, and it influences our understanding of Jesus, the gospel message, and how the Bible ought to be interpreted. In other words, the kingdom is so difficult to grasp because it is not an isolated piece of Christian thought; it stretches into nearly every aspect of the Christian life. Nichols admits that because the kingdom is integral to so many parts of the Christian life, trying to understand it in isolation is like the theological version of the chicken and the egg.[3]

Another aspect of God's kingdom that makes it difficult to understand is that pastors and teachers have emphasized different parts of it throughout history. Classical liberal theologians highlighted God's kingdom rule, located in the individual believer; thus, the manifestation of God's kingship became relative to each person. Liberation-oriented theologians highlighted the rule of God in an ethical society. Evangelicals stressed the "already/not yet" nature of the kingdom, claiming that the kingdom has already arrived, in part, via the church. At present, we await the full onset of God's kingdom that has not yet arrived but that will be established on his return to earth when he reigns over all of creation. The "already/not yet" understanding of the kingdom beautifully captures the idea that believers in the church are kingdom citizens and examples of Christ's reign in the life of the individual. Through them, God seeks to enact his plan in larger society.

The kingdom offers a universal goal for our work that sets us on a biblical trajectory, pointing us to God's life-giving rule over all creation. Scripture proclaims that the kingdom is a place where the brokenness of creation will no longer exist because God "will wipe away every tear from their eyes, and death shall be no more, neither shall there be mourning, nor crying, nor pain," because he will be victorious over the curse of sin (Rev 21:4). Followers of Christ work to demonstrate the realities of the resurrection that we already enjoy, even though the coming kingdom is not yet in full bloom. This goal is the barometer we should use to analyze the affairs of our work. It begs the question whether our work "facilitates transformation ... toward ever-greater correspondence with the coming new creation."[4]

Mission and Work

The mission of God is the biblical story that engulfs all of human history and captures God's restorative action, which concludes in his kingdom. As followers of Christ, we are commissioned to bear witness to God's restorative mission on earth. To that end, this section explores our task of proclaiming and embodying that mission on the job.

The concepts of mission (singular) and missions (plural)—previously defined in chapter 3—help to clarify the ways in which believers bear witness to God's mission on the job; let's reexamine them here for clarity's sake. "Missions" is commonly understood as referring to an event with detailed parameters—a particular location, a specific time, and a defined purpose. Within those parameters, missions includes a multitude of activities. By contrast, "mission" is a general ethos, paradigm, or disposition that governs all of life.[5]

Missions and mission are often pitted against each other, but in my estimation, these two concepts work hand-in-glove to create a robust testimony to God's mission in the workplace. Proclamation and demonstration of the gospel are essential to the Christian life and witness. The one-two punch of words and actions is revealed in Scripture, and both components are vital to participation in God's mission (John 14:11; 17:18). The tension between the two arises in part because believers are often inclined to excel in one or the other. Some believers have a more demonstration- or deed-oriented witness, in which their every action on the job is in view of eternity. Others do well in facilitating strategic Bible studies and prayer times to boldly proclaim the truths of the gospel. Together, these believers are able to amplify each other's witness and catapult their work into new dimensions of kingdom usefulness.

The manner in which work is done has the potential to be a profound witness to God's mission. A supervisor should easily discern if there is a shift that is disproportionately composed of Christian employees who work as to the Lord. Fellow employees should be drawn to that crew, because a God-honoring work environment holistically enriches its workers, resulting in that crew producing the best work possible. A work environment that generates a positive group dynamic and the best work begs for proclamation of the gospel message that nurtured it.

Because the work of our hands never leaves creation static, it's important to let God's mission alter the way we work as well as the type of jobs we take as believers. Obviously, some jobs must be excluded for believers because they run contrary to how God has designed his world to flourish. For example, a pimp objectifies those made in God's image and belittles the gift of sexuality by making it into a commodity. A drug dealer sells products that tear down the people whom Christ died to restore and, in many cases, enables harmful addictions that create physical, emotional, and relational havoc for users. And those leveraging Ponzi schemes ultimately work for their own profit, neglecting God and their neighbor in their endeavors.

Let's consider a job like custodial work. The work of a janitor is often thankless, yet companies would struggle to function without them. These unsung heroes of the office continually organize what would otherwise become chaos in the office, factory, or boardroom, and they serve other workers by keeping the workplace clean so daily operations can take place without hindrance.

While custodial work is virtuous on its own, like any job, the janitor plays a part in a larger corporation whose goals must be considered when determining if a specific janitorial position is appropriate for a believer. The custodial team at my place of employment, Southeastern Baptist Theological Seminary, plays a genuine role in fulfilling the school's mission statement of "[Seeking] to glorify the Lord Jesus Christ by equipping students to serve the Church and fulfill the Great Commission." Likewise, the janitorial team at city hall plays a part in the honorable work of shaping society as a place where citizens can flourish. Understanding the mission of God can also help the believer to determine whether an otherwise honorable job is within an organization whose goals are antithetical to God's purposes.

God might call his people into job situations as agents of reconciliation, to align an organization with his purposes. For example, there are organizations whose work is ultimately good, but the daily operations of the office or factory do not please God. He might put a believer into a position of leadership in this difficult situation to establish God-honoring practices within the company. The responsibility to bring about change is greater when employees rank higher on the company's organizational chart. Contrary to worldly wisdom, the higher their place in a company, the more God holds them responsible to serve others on the jobsite.

In the end, our vocational spheres are ground zero for proclaiming and demonstrating the kingdom and bearing testimony to God's restorative mission in the world. Among all of God's creation, people are uniquely equipped for this task. Scripture is clear that the Lord will not be without a witness, because even the rocks can cry out to God if necessary (Luke 19:40; Rom 8:22). This being the case, what makes human testimony to the Creator so unique? Building on our study of Genesis 1–2, we'll see that God's image-bearing vice-regents are exclusively commissioned to subdue and have dominion over creation (Gen 1:28).

People offer an exceptional witness to God's mission because, unlike other living beings, we are uniquely aware of both temporal and spiritual realities. Theologian Herman Bavinck says:

> [Animals] are aware of earthly but not heavenly things; they are aware of the actual, the pleasant, and the useful, but they have no notion of the true, the good, and the beautiful; they have a sensuous awareness and a sensuous desire, but they are therefore also satisfied by the sensuous and cannot penetrate through to the spiritual order.[6]

Thus, human desires cannot be met solely by the sensuous like an animal's can. Bavinck continues, locating the origin of human desires:

> This yearning for an eternal order, which God has planted in the heart of man, in the inmost recesses of his being ... is the cause of the indisputable fact that everything which belongs to the temporal order [alone] cannot satisfy man[kind].[7]

When we try to satisfy these desires while neglecting to address the earthly and spiritual together, we abandon God's plan by seeking to fulfill our desires contrary to our design; in essence, we neglect what it means to be human and cause dysfunction in our lives. We are susceptible to this trap on the job if we try to appease our desire to be successful; even if the goal is achieved, our work is not proactively intertwined with God's mission (i.e., the spiritual). This leads to discontentment that, in turn, causes us to overwork because we look to receive something from it that—isolated from God's mission—it can never deliver.

The intersection of the temporal and the spiritual in the workplace also reminds us of our salvation: When we are made new in Christ, the Holy Spirit opens our hearts and minds to the wisdom that God has inscribed into creation and reveals how our work can direct us and others toward God himself.

As spiritual beings, we have to take our spirituality into every temporal endeavor we pursue because not doing so would belittle our role as image-bearers. And by understanding our unique role in God's kingdom program, those of us who seek to equip believers to enhance their image-bearing capacity on the job must emphasize the path of discipleship.

Discipleship and Work

In my experience, intentional discipleship was primarily aimed at cultivating spiritual formation via spiritual disciplines. The primary means of growth was equipping young believers to read, interpret, and apply Scripture and proclaim the gospel to others. These tools are indispensable for the Christian life, but we seek to expand the horizons of discipleship in light of the call to wed the temporal and eternal facets of work for the kingdom's sake. We'll call this whole-life discipleship, and Greg Forster reminds us of its necessity:

> The gap between discipleship and everyday life is not only a threat to the church. It is also a major cause of the public crises that are now confronting human civilization. ... Work and the economy are critical connection points between the church and the world. When Christians manifest their faith in the life of civilization through their fruitful work and economic wisdom, they cannot help but have a profound impact on the making of human civilization. But when discipleship is disconnected from work and the economy, as it too often is now, civilization develops in other directions.[8]

Whole-life discipleship does not jettison spiritual formation, but requires it. Sanctification is a progressive inner renewal in every phase of human life. When a spirit of holiness penetrates our lives, it makes qualitative differences in the inner workings of our family, business, church, and community. The renewing power of salvation in Christ penetrates every fabric of the natural world, sanctifying it from within.[9]

Training ourselves to see the world anew is essential to the process of whole-life discipleship, which instills in us the ability to view the world through the corrective lens of Scripture. Subsequently, the Holy Spirit begins to reveal both the curse of sin throughout creation and an equally strong desire for redemption.[10] Furthermore, Scripture offers a worldview that instructs us in how to renew the brokenness the Spirit reveals. Disciples learn to ask questions such as, "What was this like before the fall?," "How has the fall affected this?," and "How can I work to restore this to its divinely intended purpose?"

While we commonly spiritualize the nature of discipleship, we approach the notion of apprenticeship as developing secular vocational skills. Whole-life discipleship helpfully integrates both discipleship and apprenticeship. Thus Christian disciples are simultaneously taught how to glorify God by loving their neighbor *and* by offering the best goods and services in a manner that aligns with God's purposes.

For the individual, whole-life discipleship seeks to mend each relationship within the Christian worldview, beginning with that between humanity and creation. Since work is what people do with creation, gainful employment involves cultivating creation in a constructive or marketable fashion. A good **relationship between humanity and creation** is imperative for Christian workers to develop robust skill sets and pass them along to others.

This type of discipleship development is done most effectively on the job. Perhaps an experienced plumber notices a novice has joined the crew; the older worker can holistical-ly develop the younger in the context of their daily work. In essence, the discipleship process brings about the hid-den potential in the inexperienced worker. Teaching some-one how to excel in a chosen field gives them an avenue to cultivate God's creation (Gen 1:28–30), thus allowing for a young worker to have dominion over creation as Christ's vice-regent.

Furthermore, employment depends on whether work-ers have good **relationships with others**. Unfortunately, some of the most gifted people with highly refined skills are jobless because of their lack of relationship skills. A voca-tional mentor can assist mentees with interpersonal skills and utilize personal relationships to help mentees find an appropriate way to exercise their skills. If the mentor wit-nesses progress and has a colleague who is hiring, she could refer the protégé to a job and vouch for the skill set that she helped develop.

Whole-life discipleship helps us cultivate a vibrant **rela-tionship with ourselves**, since working is part of reflecting God's image. Remember, we were introduced to God himself as a worker in Genesis 1:1. When we, as image-bearers, have the opportunity to work and provide for our own needs, it brings about dignity that is rooted in our ability to reflect the actions of God himself. In essence, working instills in us a sense of fulfillment and value that undergirds a healthy view of ourselves.

Finally, most foundational to whole-life discipleship is the **human relationship with God.** After having selflessly served together, a mentor has the opportunity to communicate to a mentee the message of the gospel, which then heals the one relationship that makes the others (noted above) possible. While common grace allows us some ability to rebuild these relationships, we can be truly restored with the spiritual and earthly realities only by becoming a new creation. Only after salvation can we work as being informed by the kingdom, bearing witness to God's mission, and in light of our image-bearing capacity. Workers can only experience what it means to work as to the Lord when they are followers of Christ. Following Christ is prerequisite to becoming a fulfilled worker who cultivates love for one's neighbor, peace with one's self, and an understanding of God's world.

Conclusion

Our calling, as workers, is to develop the hidden potentials in our work and in those around us with the perfection of the kingdom as our guide. The ministry that work assumes develops organizations, processes, and people; the cultural mandate demands nothing less.

Action Points

- What is the kingdom of God, and how does it inform how you think about your work?

- What is the difference between missions and mission?

- How can you integrate being a missional worker into the discipleship process?

Recommended Reading

Bavinck, Herman. *Our Reasonable Faith*. Grand Rapids: Eerdmans, 1956.

Moore, Russell. *Onward: Engaging the Culture without Losing the Gospel*. Nashville: B&H Publishing Group, 2015.

Morgan, Christopher W., and Robert A Peterson, eds. *The Kingdom of God*. Wheaton, IL: Crossway, 2012.

Forster, Greg. "Theology that Works: Making Disciples Who Practice Fruitful Work and Economic Wisdom in Modern America." The Oikonomia Network, 2013.

Bonhoeffer, Dietrich. *Discipleship*. Ed. Martin Kuske and Ilse Tödt. Trans. Barbara Green and Reinhard Krauss. Minneapolis: Fortress Press, 2001.

The Way Forward

So where do we go from here? It can be easy to walk away from a book like this without a clear idea of how to implement its ideas into daily life. And, indeed, implementation will look different for each vocation. Nevertheless, here are three categories of suggestions for how to begin incorporating an *every-waking-hour* mindset into your daily life at work and beyond.

Recalling a Biblical Understanding of Work

Work is what people do with creation. Vocation is the way or ways we make ourselves useful to others. Further, work is the hand that animates the glove of our vocations.

God, in his wisdom, designed his world to be managed by people—who are made in his image. Our work is part of that management or stewardship of God's world. Engaging in any activity means that we interact with God's creation, and inevitably we direct it toward him or away from him. Our work either promotes God's way in his world or it promotes folly. This is true in every part of life to which we're called.

Integrating our faith into our work begins by considering the starting place, the ending place (or *telos*), and the way in between. Proverbs 1:7 and 9:10 teach that the beginning of all proper knowledge and wisdom is the fear of the Lord. Crossing this threshold of awe requires humility and the proper perspective that God is God and we are not. Thus, the journey of our lives—including our work—begins with the confession of faith in the Lord Christ and the commitment to walk in his way (Deut 10:12).

Next we establish the end goal of the twin loves of God and neighbor. Loving God and others is always right; hence Jesus identified them as the greatest commandments. As such, they must inform our every kind of work. Asking, "How do I best love God and others in my work?" is sure to point us in the right direction for incorporating our faith and our work. Further, this question, if carefully considered, will help us avoid the general application of loving our neighbor and, instead, offer a very specific application of these twin loves in our interactions with each person, time, place, and vocation.

Only after establishing the proper beginning and end of our work can we consider the way in between. The "way of righteousness" stretches across the whole of our lives. We walk the way of the one who is the way, truth, and life— the one known as a carpenter before we knew him as Christ. This way informs our engagement with God, others, ourselves, and with the rest of creation. As stewards of God's world, we must apply the way of righteousness to all of culture—business, politics, landscaping, economics, education, engineering, technology, art, family, medicine, and beyond—and through every vocation.

I (Benjamin) recognize at least five callings, or vocations, in my own life. I am called to Christ, my family, my church, my job of teaching, and my neighborhood. Each of these requires *work*, though I receive a paycheck for only one of them. Nevertheless, at any given time I am engaging God's world (working) through one or more of these vocations, and I pray that the work of my hands, feet, mind, and mouth promotes the way of God.

Finally, we must recall the role of faith in our work. We believe that our salvation in Christ comes by grace through faith, which is a gift from God (Eph 2:8-9). Further, as Ephesians 2:10 teaches, we are created *for good works*. These come as a result of the gift of faith, and we believe these good works aren't merely spiritual. As material beings who are responsible for God's material world, we can reasonably conclude that the Spirit's power working within us extends both to spiritual and physical work. In light of this, for every activity of life, we perform Paul's words from 1 Corinthians 10:31: "Whether you eat or drink, or whatever you do, do all to the glory of God."

Church Leadership that Integrates the Gospel and Work

Church leaders play a major role in helping Christians understand their role as ministers in God's economy of all things. Here are seven suggestions for how pastors, in particular, might consider their role in relation to the workers in the congregation.

First, reconsider what it means to "equip the saints for the work of ministry" (Eph 4:12). Paul's reference to "the saints" here refers not to pastors, teachers, and those already named in 4:11, but to the saints in the pews who also bear the title "minister." What is their ministry? Is it service to local congregations? It certainly isn't less than that, but we believe it also stretches beyond our local congregations to build up the kingdom at large. These are gifts in business, education, leadership, woodworking, art, homemaking, and beyond—all areas that fall under the purview of Christ's kingdom and ache for gifted saints to apply the ways of the King. Must the pastor, then, become an expert in his parishioner's vocations? No, but perhaps he could begin by considering "equipping the saints" with Monday's cubicle in mind rather than just Sunday's small group.

Second, consider tweaking your language to include all believers in the ministerial roster. In addition to Ephesians 4:12, 2 Corinthians 5:18 further reinforces that every member is a minister in the body of Christ, yet the divide between pastor and pew remains wide in many churches. This divide can—and should—be narrowed, however, by reminding all saints of their role as Christian ministers in their workplaces. This means that the sacred nature of Sunday stretches into Monday through Saturday, invading every waking hour, every place and activity. Work must be valued as intrinsically good and meaningful, not merely as a means to evangelism and missions. Indeed, sharing Christ with coworkers is critical, but we must also step up our rhetoric about Christian excellence, stewardship, and faithfulness in the believer's vocational responsibilities.

Third, emphasize the ministry of the saints as more than spiritual work. Recall the Dorothy Sayers quote from her essay "Why Work?," discussed in chapter 3, and consider how this way of thinking might empower your people in their work.

Fourth, visit your parishioners at work. What signals respect and appreciation for a parishioner's work as much as a pastoral visit to the classroom, dealership, warehouse, or farm? Further, when it comes to understanding and addressing problems at work, pastors are far better equipped to offer wisdom in complicated circumstances when they have encountered people's workplaces. Consider building time into your weekly schedule to visit one workplace per week, and get to know the work—i.e., the ministry—of your saints.

Fifth, ask questions that help the saints see how their work fits into God's grand economy. If it's true that saints who are not pastors, preachers, prophets, apostles, and teachers are *in* the ministry, and if it's true that Christ created *all* things and has authority over *all* things, then how is the variety of vocations represented in our congregation contributing to and participating in the mission of God? How does each job promote all things good, true, beautiful, just, right, and wise—both spiritually and physically? Asking and answering such questions reveal meaning and intrinsic value in vocations.[1] What a service we offer to our fellow believers when we help them see why their work matters!

Sixth, pray publicly for saints in all vocations. Churches often pray publicly for missionaries and church planters as they're sent out by the church to serve another people and place. But why do we seldom pray for the rest of the ministers in the congregation? We're not suggesting that churches discontinue public prayer for pastors and missionaries but that they include prayer for the mechanics, mail carriers, police officers, fire fighters, artists, politicians, and educators as they, too, perform their ministerial duties. As one local church in North Carolina prayed for public school teachers at the beginning of this school year, I noticed tears in the eyes of several of these faithful men and women preparing to return to their ministries in the classroom.

Finally, offer resources and opportunities for your people to further connect their forms of ministry with God's mission in the world. Dozens of good books, websites, and centers exist to promote the integration of faith and work.[2] But let us not stop with recommendations. Consider how to infuse these discussions into the life of your church through Sunday school, small groups, sermon applications, and missions efforts.

Training the Next Generation with a Proper Understanding of Work

Helping the next generation think properly about faith and work is imperative. Pages of children's books and curriculum on this topic deserve to be written by far more competent authors. Nonetheless, from one parent to others, here are five ideas for teaching children and teens a healthy view of work and calling.

First, we must echo Jesus' words that the most important thing about living in God's world is loving God and loving others. If this is true, it is the sure direction for all of life, and it is impossible to overstate.

Second, we should affirm their gifts and abilities as given by God and capable of promoting God's way in the world. Western culture emphasizes athletic, musical, and academic abilities. But could we also make much of the gifts of encouragement, hospitality, administration, leadership, creativity, construction, science, teaching, and beyond? These—and many more—gifts are also God-given and useful for promoting God's kingdom on earth as it is in heaven.

Third, we can encourage curiosity in the goodness of both the spiritual and physical aspects of God's world. Scripture teaches that the world was built by wisdom, which is wrought into the warp and woof of creation. Thus, by observing creation, we can learn about the Creator and how to live. We must always be on guard against worshiping the creation over the Creator; however, assuming properly ordered worship, we can be encouraged to investigate, understand, and cultivate God's world.

Fourth, we can lead our kids to memorize 2 Corinthians 5:17-18: "Therefore, if anyone is in Christ, he is a new creation. The old has passed away; behold, the new has come. All this is from God, who through Christ reconciled us to himself and gave us the ministry of reconciliation." Keeping these verses together reminds us of the ministerial call of every believer. Indeed, every Christian dons the clerical collar.

Fifth, we must teach our children the importance of both evangelism and mission. By evangelism, I mean the verbal sharing of the gospel of Christ with those who haven't heard or believed it before. By mission, I mean the manner of living that accords with the good news that Jesus is king, now and forever. Both telling of Christ with our mouths and giving Christ with our hands and feet characterize this life on mission. It isn't "either/or," it's "both/and."

May this be merely the beginning of the ever-important conversation about how to transfer truth to the next generation, and may that transfer begin with our own children and grandchildren.

With Whom Should We Work?
A Framework for
Collaboration

In essentials, unity; in doubtful matters,
liberty; in all things, charity.[1]

—POPE JOHN XXIII

Several years ago, I (Benjamin) enjoyed a tour of historic Oxford, England, led by theologian and C. S. Lewis expert Jeanette Sears. Dr. Sears' tour showcased Oxford from the perspective of the Inklings, the famous club of friends made up of Lewis, J. R. R. Tolkien, Charles Williams, and Owen Barfield, among others. Our tour for the day concluded at the Inklings' favorite meeting place, the Eagle and Child pub (known by locals as "the Bird and Baby") where today a plaque and a few pictures hang in their honor.

As we approached the Eagle and Child, someone asked Dr. Sears, "Wasn't Lewis Anglican?" Dr. Sears affirmed that it was true. "And wasn't Tolkien Catholic?" Dr. Sears affirmed again. "With such religious differences, how were they able to come together and collaborate in their work?" Dr. Sears quickly responded, "Because they committed early on to focus on their agreements, not their differences."

When Christians become intentional about integrating their faith and their work, many believers find questions quickly emerge about collaborating with others. I often receive questions from Baptists about whether it is okay to collaborate with Methodists or Presbyterians to begin a morning Bible study at work. And I've heard more than a few Baptists comment that they cannot even consider collaborating with Anglicans or Catholics—though they're unsure why. For some, this feels silly and ignorant. For others, however, it is serious and born from the honest desire to honor Christ.

We suggest that Christians can and should collaborate with believers of other Christian traditions and, at times, with other religions or the nonreligious—*toward righteous ends.* We will call collaboration with other Christian traditions "missional" and collaboration with other religions and the nonreligious "moral." Missional collaboration connects to the term catholicity,[2] while moral collaboration is concerned with the moral solidarity that Christians sometimes share with other religions or with those who have no religious affiliation.

Ultimately, this appendix will offer a model for catholicity and solidarity. We will begin by first, remembering the goal of our work; second, stressing the importance of awareness of what others are already doing; and third, considering what missional and moral collaboration might look like at work and beyond.

Pope John XXIII, in his 1959 encyclical *Ad Petri Cathedram*, included the quote in the epigraph above: "In essentials, unity; in doubtful matters, liberty; in all things, charity." Such is the spirit of this section. By no means do we suggest that Christians should relinquish core convictions for the sake of collaboration. On the contrary, we believe that core Christian convictions stem from historic Christian orthodoxy and therefore transcend denomination and tradition. These common convictions thus pave the way for missional collaboration. Moreover, core Christian convictions are often charged with moral imperatives to promote love, justice, and mercy in the workplace and beyond. Such expressions are sometimes shared by other religions or by the nonreligious, thus providing opportunities for moral collaboration *toward righteous ends.*

The *end* to which we collaborate must be clear from the beginning to protect against doctrinal demise. Thus, we begin by recalling the *telos* of our work in God's world.

Keeping the Goal in View

As discussed in chapter 4, the *telos* (end or goal) of the Christian life is multifaceted. To begin, if the architect of all things—God—insists that the most important thing about living in his world is to love him and love others, this must serve as the *end* to which we work. Indeed, this One through whom all things were made (John 1:3) is himself the "end [*telos*] of the law" (Rom 10:4), and he is the one we are called to "grow up in" (Eph 4:15) as we mature in Christlikeness.

As we work, then, we must direct every task, relationship, responsibility, meeting, and water-cooler conversation to the end of double love of God and neighbor. This begins by simply asking the question, "What does Great Commandment–inspired love look like right now?" Such a question echoes the words of Jesus as he taught us to pray to the Father, "Your kingdom come, your will be done, on earth as it is in heaven" (Matt 6:10). By living as a kingdom citizen in the here and now, we demonstrate love for God and neighbor in every area of life—not least at work. Moreover, as our love for God and neighbor grows in word and deed, the fragrance of Christ spreads to both believers and unbelievers around us (2 Cor 2:15), and we pray that both are drawn to the King to walk faithfully with him forever.

Word and Deed

With the *telos* in sight, then, we do well to look for collaborative opportunities toward these ends, both in word and deed. Everyone's work environment is different, of course, but what opportunities can you find around you? Most opportunities fall into either the missional category with potential for evangelism, discipleship, and the communal exhortation to walk faithfully with Christ, or they fall into the moral category of advocating for and promoting love, justice, mercy, goodness, truth, and beauty.

Missional opportunities may look like a weekly prayer time or a Bible study over lunch for both believers and unbelievers. By God's grace, many have been converted to Christ through such efforts, and many more have been encouraged in their faith and reenergized in their work. Missional collaboration also takes the form of faithfulness in our deeds—our material labors. Christians—evangelicals in particular—have a healthy history of prayer breakfasts and lunchtime Bible studies sponsored by men and women in the workplace—a history I'm deeply encouraged by. But we have a poor history of promoting excellence in our work.

My mom has worked more than 25 years in the human resources division of a Fortune 100 company, and by virtue of her position, she sees both the best and worst of people. She has often told me, "You'd be surprised how Christians act at work. Some of the godliest people I know at church are not the same people during the week."

My heart sank the first time I heard this. Christians should be the best employees in the labor force. Companies should be banging on the doors of the church seeking to hire as many Christ-followers as possible. Because of high Christian character and integrity? Yes, but that's not all. It should also be because Christians do the best work. Dorothy Sayers' words ring true again where she writes, "No piety in the worker will compensate for work that is not true to itself; for any work that is untrue to its own technique is a living lie."[3]

Christian work should be known as hard and true, attending both to efficiency and excellence in the craft. When asked for one thing that really bothers him, a competition barbecue chef replied, "Barbecue restaurants that serve cheap and bland barbecue. Folks that ain't got no appreciation for the craft." I "amened" his answer and was even more encouraged to learn that he is a Christ-follower. May his tribe increase in every vocation—especially in the barbecue industry!

Awareness of Others

In his book *God at Work*, David Miller traces the development of the "Faith at Work" movement. Pope Leo XIII's encyclical *Rerum Novarum* on capital and labor, published in 1891, serves as Miller's starting point for tracing the movement's history in three waves: the Social Gospel era (1890s–1945), the ministry of the laity (1946–1980), and the Faith at Work era (1980s–present).[4]

One of the most impressive aspects of Miller's work is his presentation of breadth of the Faith at Work movement. Dozens, even hundreds, of denominational entities, parachurch organizations, nonprofit groups, Christian coalitions, seminaries, and local churches have developed strategic ministries and initiatives to bridge the gap between Sunday and Monday. Some, such as the Business as Mission movement,[5] focus broadly, while others, such as Christian Chefs International,[6] focus more specifically. We've organized just a few of them here to illustrate the extent of the movement.[7]

Colleges and Universities

- Princeton University—Faith & Work Initiative

- Yale University—Center for Faith & Culture; Ethics
  & Spirituality in the Workplace Program; Volf's book,
  Work in the Spirit: Toward a Theology of Work

Seminaries

- Southeastern Baptist Theological Seminary

- Gordon-Conwell Theological Seminary—Mockler
  Center for Faith & Ethics in the Workplace

- Bethel Seminary—Work with Purpose Initiative

- Phillips Theological Seminary—Faith &
  Work Initiative

- Dallas Theological Seminary—"Your Work: More
  Than a Paycheck" Conference

Organizations

- Cru (Campus Crusade)—Priority Associates, aimed
  at business leaders

- YWAM—Business as Mission

- InterVarsity—Marketplace Ministry;
  MBA Ministries

- The Navigators—NavWorkplace

- Oikonomia Network (Kern funded)—http://oikono-mianetwork.org

- Act3 Network

- Corporate Chaplains of America

- C12 Group

- Billy Graham Training Center—Christian Executive Leadership Forum

- The CEO Institute

- Woodstock Business Conference

Denominational Efforts

- Leagtus (Catholic)

- Mennonite Economic Development Associates (and their magazine, *The Marketplace*)

Churches

- Redeemer Presbyterian Church, New York, New York—Center for Faith & Work

- St. Mark's Episcopal Church, San Antonio, Texas—St. Benedict's Workshop

Websites

- http://www.theologyofwork.org

- http://www.oikonomianetwork.org

- http://www.faithandwork.com

- http://www.washingtoninst.org

- http://tifwe.org

Our prayer is that many readers will be motivated to integrate their faith at work with greater thoughtfulness and intentionality. Some may desire to begin a new ministry at their workplace. Others might initiate a strategy at their local church that gathers people from a variety of vocations to begin discussing how their faith intersects with their work and how they can more intentionally wield their work (i.e., their ministry) in the service of double love of God and neighbor. Whatever the initiative—and the options are endless—it is important to keep at least two things in mind.

First, the restoration of the world does not rest exclusively on our shoulders or on the effect of our ministries. It's a sobering but liberating fact that Jesus doesn't need us to accomplish his purposes in the world. In his grace, he has chosen to use us in manifold ways to model and spread the good news of the kingdom, but he doesn't *need* us. In light of this, we must remain humble with respect to our work and ministry, always careful that *our* kingdoms do not attempt to eclipse Christ's kingdom.

Second, there are likely other people and ministries already underway that overlap with the mission of your work and ministry. By nature, we—especially Americans—often allow our competitive natures to flare when we discover that others already occupy space in our "ministry market." In most cases, there is more than enough space for multiple initiatives to exist, but there is also collaboration potential that goes untapped due to ignorance, territorial feelings, pride, and so on. We want Christians to be aware of the many initiatives, institutes, ministries, centers, businesses, etc., that already exist for the purpose of kingdom impact. Our first response to these should not be competitive vexation. Rather, we should be encouraged by the prospect of colaborers and friends with wisdom and experience from which we can learn. We exhort Christians to be open to collaboration when possible. And when it is not possible or best to collaborate with other like-minded work/ministry groups, resolve to pray for and encourage the others as they labor for the kingdom.

But with whom can we collaborate? On what grounds and to what ends is it acceptable to stretch beyond our denominational, traditional, and religious boundaries? How do we approach these decisions?

An Approach to Missional and Moral Collaboration

Catholicity—Missional Collaboration

At least two modes of collaboration exist for Christians: missional and moral. Missional collaboration corresponds to catholicity, which agrees to work across denominational or traditional lines for the sake of accomplishing Christ's mission in the world. We use the term "catholic" strategically here to denote the doctrinal core around which missional collaboration can revolve.

There are countless examples of so-called missional collaboration efforts that jettisoned doctrinal fidelity for the sake of unity or some other issue. We believe, however, that missional collaboration works best when those involved agree to make doctrine central—rather than peripheral—to the collaborative effort. How can we accomplish this when working across denominational lines? By looking to the past and rallying around the ancient confessions of our faith.

The Apostles' Creed, for example, dates to the late fourth century and provides central tenets of the Christian faith:

> I believe in God, the Father almighty, creator of heaven and earth. I believe in Jesus Christ, his only Son, our Lord, who was conceived by the Holy Spirit and born of the virgin Mary. He suffered under Pontius Pilate, was crucified, died, and was buried; he descended to hell. The third day he rose again from the dead. He ascended to heaven and is seated at the right hand of God the Father almighty. From there he will come to judge the living and the dead. I believe in the Holy Spirit, the holy Catholic Church, the communion of saints, the forgiveness of sins, the resurrection of the body, and the life everlasting. Amen.

John Armstrong, in his book, *Your Church Is Too Small*, argues passionately for Christian unity that finds common ground in the past. He writes:

> New patterns of Christian faith and life are emerging in the church. I welcome these patterns, but I believe they desperately need to be rooted in the past—the creeds, the Word of God understood as the story of grace, life as a sacramental mystery, and deeply rooted spiritual formation. My thesis is simple: *The road to the future must run through the past.* My friend, the late Robert Webber, called it "ancient future faith." I share his perspective because the church must be rooted in the past and the future.[8]

The Apostles' Creed and the Nicene Creed provide a core of Christian beliefs that anchors all followers of Christ in the "faith that was once for all delivered to the saints" (Jude 1:3). These are nonnegotiables of the faith. They do not make a believer Baptist, Presbyterian, or Anglican—they make a Christian a Christian. Roman Catholic, Orthodox, and Protestant churches all agree on these core doctrines. Armstrong argues, "When core orthodoxy, as represented by the Apostles' Creed, is not of primary importance, the result will always be a small view of the church."[9] With such fundamental unity between us, and with the echo of Jesus' prayer for unity in John 17 ringing in our ears, we believe missional collaboration is not merely possible, but imperative.

These core doctrines also illuminate the boundaries of missional collaboration. To partner with someone or some organization that claims to be Christian yet denies the deity of Christ, for example, would not only be unwise, it would be fundamentally un-Christian. Such a person or group may be a potential *moral* collaborator, as we will discuss below, but they could not be a *missional* collaborator. Someone who denies Christ's deity worships a different Christ than the one to whom the apostles testify.

In saying this, we do not mean to minimize the importance of denominational distinctives. We are keenly aware of the church's history and the many godly men and women who fought for particular views of baptism, the Eucharist, and beyond. However, Jesus' prayer in John 17 compels Christians to unity whenever and wherever possible for the sake of Christ, his kingdom, and his mission in the world.

Solidarity—Moral Collaboration[10]

A close friend and entrepreneur recently shared with me that he is partnering with an American-based billionaire to address issues related to world hunger and sex trafficking. "I'm a little nervous about it, though," he said. When I asked why, he said, "Because the guy I'm partnering with is Hindu." My friend explained that at first he was uncomfortable partnering with someone of another religion, but he ultimately found comfort in their mutual desires to see hunger and sex trafficking eliminated.

By the end of our conversation, I affirmed and encouraged my friend in his partnership. Such a partnership decision is not as easy as agreeing on the *ends*, though. Simple pragmatism has landed more than a few decision-makers—and policy-makers—in trouble. In addition to the ends, it is also important to consider the motives, means, methods, and manner. Each serves as an integral and irreducible part of the whole.

Concerning motives, moral collaboration and partnership should aim in the same direction—that is, in the direction of the *other*. Others-centeredness is the stuff of virtue. Double love of God and neighbor aims our wants (i.e., desires) away from ourselves and toward others. Moral collaborators should agree to work for the good of others, not for the sole good of themselves.

Means and methods work together as the material execution of the collaborative effort. You have doubtless heard it said, "The ends do not justify the means," and indeed they do not. Dr. Martin Luther King, Jr., rightly insisted, "The means we use must be as pure as the ends we seek."[11] Moral collaboration must consider this important truth. It must avoid the temptation to employ vicious means and methods to accomplish virtuous ends. Double love of God and neighbor speaks just as directly to how creatures and creation are treated along the way (means and methods) as to the ends of things.

Finally, manner must be considered integral to moral collaboration. Faith, hope, and charity (love) are expected of those who follow Christ. Particularly, faith and hope are anchored in true faith in the true God and are gifted to the people of God. Charity seems unique, however, with respect to moral collaboration. The faith and hope of non-Christian collaborators is located somewhere other than in the person of Jesus Christ and his work of reconciling the world to himself (2 Cor 5:17–19). Their charity, however, seems more congruent with that of the Christian. Even if fundamentally disordered, the others-centered love of the non-Christian, especially when joined to the work of Christians, serves to promote goodness, truth, and beauty in God's world. We understand this to be a result of God's common grace on fallen creatures—the Schindler effect, if you will. Such works of charity are not understood to be salvific in any way, but do they promote good in God's world? We think so.

To be sure, as with other sections in this book, this appendix is merely the beginning of the conversation. Much wisdom and discernment is required when partnering with others for either missional or moral purposes. At the very least, however, we pray that this will provide helpful categories for furthering the conversation and promoting the justice, mercy, love, goodness, truth, and beauty of God in his world.

Vocation Questions

One aim of this book is to help readers connect the dots between their faith and their work. Along the way, we framed a biblical worldview encompassing the whole of God's world, including the workplace.

However, our efforts in this book are only the beginning of the conversation. We neither know the specifics of every job, nor are we experts in every (any!) job. So what more have we to offer?

In this appendix, we move from the sweeping concept of worldview to specific questions about work. We designed these questions to stir your imagination to creatively connect your faith to the specifics of your work.

We don't intend for answering these questions to be a rigid science, but rather an art that helps you unearth the unique missional possibilities of your work. Although they are helpful for an individual, the best results are likely to emerge from a Spirit-filled community of workers in similar fields of work.

The Nuts and Bolts of Your Job

1. What are the details of your job description?

2. Do you execute the responsibilities in your job description faithfully and with excellence? How?

3. Where is your job located on the organizational chart?

4. What does considering the interests of others above your own (Phil 2:3) look like in your role? What about for those below, above, and beside you on the organizational chart?

Your Job's Place in the Whole

1. What is the mission (or goal) of your company, and how does your job contribute to those objectives?

2. How can you build camaraderie at work by helping others understand their work in light of the company's overall mission?

3. How does your job and organization fit into the web of relationships we call the economy?

4. How does your work contribute to flourishing in God's world (providing food, electricity, education, etc.)?

Theological Integration

1. Which of the four human relationships are prominent in your work (God, others, self or creation)?

2. How has the fall affected your work? (Consider the four relationships above.)

3. How might you work to redirect sin's effects?

4. Do you detect injustices in your workplace? How might you advocate for justice and righteousness in a wise and loving way?

5. What theological themes are prominent in your work?

6. How does Scripture inform the values of your work?

Recommended Reading Summary

Asmus, Barry, and Wayne Grudem. *The Poverty of Nations: A Sustainable Solution*. Wheaton, IL: Crossway, 2013. An economic and theological attempt to offer a solution to the issue of the poverty of the nations.

Ballor, Jordan. *Ecumenical Babel: Confusing Economic Ideology and the Church's Social Witness*. Grand Rapids: Christian's Library Press, 2010. A critical examination of how the ecumenical movement has dealt with ethical and economic issues.

Berghoef, Gerard, and Lester Dekoster. *Faithful in All God's House: Stewardship and the Christian Life*. Grand Rapids: Christian's Library Press, 2013. A short introduction to stewardship that illustrates what biblical stewardship looks like in the Christian life.

Bolt, John. *Economic Shalom: A Reformed Primer on Faith, Work and Human Flourishing*. Grand Rapids: Christian's Library Press, 2013. A primer on faith, work, and human flourishing from a Reformed perspective.

Bradley, Anne, and Art Lindsley, eds. *For the Least of These: A Biblical Answer to Poverty*. Bloomington, IN: WestBow Press, 2014. Provides biblical and economic perspectives of poverty and promotes wise stewardship principles to enable society to flourish.

Brand, Chad. *Flourishing Faith: A Baptist Primer on Work, Economics and Civic Stewardship*. Grand Rapids: Christian's Library Press, 2012. An accessible introduction to work, economics, and civic stewardship.

The Call of the Entrepreneur. Directed by Simon Scionka. Acton Media, 2007. A documentary about three entrepreneurs that shows how to view the role of entrepreneurs in the economy and in the world.

Claar, Victor, and Robin Klay. *Economics in Christian Perspective: Theory, Policy and Life Choices*. Downers Grove, IL: InterVarsity Press, 2007. An in-depth look at economics theory and policy from a Christian viewpoint to further human flourishing.

Cleveland, Drew, and Greg Forster, eds. *The Pastor's Guide to Fruitful Work and Economic Wisdom: Understanding What Your People Do All Day*. Made to Flourish, 2012. A collection of essays designed to help equip pastors to understand the connection between ministry and work of the people in the congregation.

Corbett, Steve, and Brian Fikkert. *When Helping Hurts: How to Alleviate Poverty without Hurting the Poor ... and Yourself*. Chicago: Moody, 2012. A foundational discussion on the nature of poverty that explains best practices for implementing poverty-alleviation strategies without hurting the poor or the helpers.

Crouch, Andy. *Culture Making: Recovering Our Creative Calling.* Downers Grove, IL: InterVarsity Press, 2008. A manifesto calling Christians to be creators of culture and to participate in God's work in culture.

DeKoster, Lester. *Work: The Meaning of Your Life.* Grand Rapids: Christian's Library Press, 2010. A short work examining how work gives meaning to life.

For the Life of the World: Letters to the Exiles. Directed by Eric Johnson and David Michael Phelps. Grand Rapids: Acton Institute, 2015. A seven-episode DVD looking at how to contribute to the life of the world in prosperity and flourishing as well as one's place in the mission of God.

Forster, Greg. *Joy for the World: How Christianity Lost its Cultural Influence & Can Begin to Rebuild it.* Wheaton, IL: Crossway, 2014. A look at the relationship between Christianity and culture in America and what cultural influence and transformation looks like.

Garber, Steven. *Visions of Vocation: Common Grace for the Common Good.* Downers Grove, IL: InterVarsity Press, 2014. An invitation to Christians to see themselves care for the flourishing of the world.

Guinness, Os. *The Call: Finding and Fulfilling the Central Purpose of your Life.* Nashville: Nelson, 2003. A modern classic examining the answers to identity, meaning, and purpose.

Gwartney, James, Richard Stroup, and Dwight Lee. *Common Sense Economics: What Everyone Should Know about Wealth and Prosperity.* New York: St. Martin's Press, 2005. A basic introduction to economics with examples of how the principles work on the large scale and the personal level.

Keller, Timothy. *Every Good Endeavor*. New York: Dutton, 2012. An extensive look at a Christian view of work.

Kuyper, Abraham. *Wisdom & Wonder: Common Grace in Science and Art*. Ed. Jordan J. Ballor and Stephen J. Grabill. Trans. Nelson D. Kloosterman. Bellingham, WA: Lexham Press, 2015. An introduction to Kuyper's doctrine of common grace, specifically examining the realms of science and art.

Miller, David. *God at Work: The History and Promise of the Faith at Work Movement*. Oxford: Oxford University Press, 2007. A historical examination and analysis of the faith at work movement in the United States.

Nelson, Tom. *Work Matters: Connecting Sunday Worship to Monday Work*. Wheaton, IL: Crossway, 2011. An accessible look at how Christians should relate the call to work to the call to follow Christ.

Placher, William, ed. *Callings: Twenty Centuries of Christian Wisdom on Vocation*. Grand Rapids: Eerdmans, 2005. A collection of essays from church history on work and vocation; a good overview of the topic from the life of the church.

Richards, Jay. *Money, Greed and God: Why Capitalism Is the Solution and Not the Problem*. New York: HarperOne, 2009. An examination of why Christians can and should work within a capitalist system to help the world flourish.

Sayers, Dorothy. *The Mind of the Maker*. New York: HarperOne, 1941. A classic work examining creativity through the lens of the doctrine of the Trinity.

Schneider, John. *The Good of Affluence: Seeking God in a Culture of Wealth*. Grand Rapids: Eerdmans, 2002. A theological work written to help Christians find God in a capitalist culture of wealth.

Sherman, Amy. *Kingdom Calling: Vocational Stewardship for the Common Good*. Downers Grove, IL: InterVarsity Press, 2011. An examination of vocational stewardship and how it offers a way to advance the kingdom mission.

Sirico, Robert. *The Call of the Entrepreneur*. Grand Rapids: Acton Institute, 2007. A study guide that supplements *The Call of the Entrepreneur* DVD and delves into some topics the DVD does not cover.

——. *Defending the Free Market: The Moral Case for a Free Economy*. Washington, D.C.: Regnery Publishing, 2012. A moral argument for capitalism and a free-market system.

Stevens, R. Paul. *Work Matters: Lessons from Scripture*. Grand Rapids: Eerdmans, 2012. A condensed biblical theology of work.

Teevan, John Addison. *Integrated Justice and Equality: Biblical Wisdom for Those Who Do Good Works*. Grand Rapids: Christian's Library Press, 2014. Encourages Christians to adopt the idea of integrated justice in their gospel mission.

Van Duzer, Jeff. *Why Business Matters to God: And What Still Needs to Be Fixed*. Downers Grove, IL: InterVarsity Press, 2010. Presents business as a kingdom-advancing calling and proposes some changes to existing business practices.

Veith, Gene, Jr. *God at Work: Your Christian Vocation in All of Life*. Wheaton, IL: Crossway, 2002. A spiritual framework for understanding the doctrine of vocation and how it applies everyday life.

Volf, Miroslav. *Work in the Spirit*. Eugene, OR: Wipf and Stock, 2001. A look at work from the perspective of the doctrine of the Holy Spirit; presents a different view than the traditional Protestant understanding of the doctrine of vocation.

Whelchel, Hugh. *How then Shall We Work? Rediscovering the Biblical Doctrine of Work*. Bloomington, IN: WestBow Press, 2012. A brief biblical and historical theology of work that concludes with what work means for Christians today.

Witherington, Ben, III. *Work: A Kingdom Perspective on Labor*. Grand Rapids: Eerdmans, 2011. A theological examination of work with an emphasis on how work relates to the eschatological understanding of the kingdom.

Introduction

1. John R. W. Stott, *The Message of Ephesians* (Downers Grove, IL: IVP Academic, 1984), iii.
2. Most of the chapters were written exclusively by Walter or Benjamin, and we have sought to indicate this by parenthetically inserting the appropriate name after an initial first person pronoun. Chapters 1 and 2, however, contain content from both authors, though Walter was the primary architect for these.
3. Business consultant Matthew May notes that virtually every design school professor and graphic designer with a blog has commented on the FedEx logo during their careers. Matthew May, "The Story Behind the Famous FedEx Logo, and Why It Works," *Fast Company Blog*, October 23, 2012, http://www.fastcodesign.com/1671067/the-story-behind-the-famous-fedex-logo-and-why-it-works.
4. Illustration borrowed from a conversation with Hugh Whelchel on May 1, 2014.

Chapter 1: Theology of Work

1. Note both that work goes beyond people (ants, for example, work; see Prov 30:25) and that our definition of work is strictly from the perspective of one of God's creatures—we fully recognize that God himself also works.
2. Modified from Lester Dekoster's definition of work in *Work: The Meaning of Your Life; A Christian Perspective*.
3. Gordon Spykman, *Reformational Theology: A New Paradigm for Doing Dogmatics* (Grand Rapids: Eerdmans, 1992), 66–67.
4. Russell Moore, "The Doctrine of the Last Things," in *A Theology for the Church* (Nashville: B&H, 2007), 858.

5. Christopher J. H. Wright, *The Mission of God's People: A Biblical Theology of the Church's Mission* (Grand Rapids: Zondervan, 2010), 39.
6. Wright, *The Mission of God's People,* 40.
7. Robert J. Banks, *Faith Goes to Work: Reflections from the Marketplace* (Eugene, Wiph and Stock, 1999). My summary of the divine characteristics listed in Bank's work is influenced by Amy Sherman's interpretation of them in her book *Kingdom Calling* (103-04).

Chapter 2: Work throughout the Old Testament

1. Chad Brand, *Flourishing Faith: A Baptist Primer on Work, Economics and Civic Stewardship* (Grand Rapids: Christian's Library Press, 2012), 2.
2. David H. Jensen, *Responsive Labor: A Theology of Work* (Louisville, KY: Westminster John Knox Press, 2006), 22.
3. Timothy Keller, *Every Good Endeavor: Connecting Your Work to God's Work* (New York: Dutton, 2012), 48.
4. Chad Brand, *Flourishing Faith: A Baptist Primer on Work, Economics, and Civic Stewardship* (Grand Rapids: Christian's Library Press, 2012), 3.
5. Albert Wolters, *Creation Regained: Biblical Basics for a Reformational Worldview* 2nd edition (Grand Rapids: Eerdmans, 2005), 41-42.
6. Timothy Keller, *Every Good Endeavor: Connecting Your Work to God's Work* (New York: Dutton, 2012), 41.
7. John Piper, *Don't Waste Your Life* (Wheaton, IL: Crossway, 2003), 36.
8. Craig G. Bartholomew and Ryan P. O'Dowd, *Old Testament Wisdom Literature: A Theological Introduction* (Downers Grove, IL: IVP Academic, 2011), 104.

Chapter 3: Work throughout the New Testament

1. Dorothy Sayers, "Why Work?," in *Letters to a Diminished Church: Passionate Arguments for the Relevance of Christian Doctrine* (Nashville: W Publishing Group, 2004), 132.
2. For a fuller treatment of work in the New Testament, see R. Paul Stevens' *Work Matters: Lessons from Scripture* (Grand Rapids: Eerdmans, 2012).
3. Dorothy Sayers, "Why Work?," in *Letters to a Diminished Church*, 131-32.
4. More precisely, the idiom "Gird up your loins!" or "Be dressed in readiness!" (NASB).

5. This is the same kind of "blessedness" seen in the beatitudes of Matt 5:3–10.
6. The word for "manager" here is *oikonomos*, the personalized form of *oikonomia*, from which comes the English word "economics." The imagery is that of a well-ordered household, with the *oikonomos* (manager) being the person in charge.
7. Abraham Kuyper, from his inaugural address at the dedication of the Free University. Found in James D. Bratt, *Abraham Kuyper: A Centennial Reader* (Grand Rapids: Eerdmans, 1998), 488.
8. For a fuller treatment, see Robert Harvey and Philip H. Towner, *2 Peter and Jude* in *The IVP New Testament Commentary Series* (Downers Grove, IL: IVP Academic, 2009).

Chapter 4: Christ, Wisdom, and Work

1. Augustine, *On Free Choice of the Will*, trans. Thomas Williams (Indianapolis: Hackett Publishing Company, 1993), 61–62.
2. For more on how wisdom appears in the Bible and other literature of the ancient Near East, see Martin A. Shields, "Wisdom," in *Lexham Bible Dictionary* (Bellingham, WA: Lexham Press, 2015).
3. See chapter 3, "Work throughout the New Testament," for more.
4. Augustine, *On Free Choice of the Will*, trans. Thomas Williams (Indianapolis: Hackett Publishing Company, 1993), 61–62.
5. See Al Wolters' *Creation Regained* (Grand Rapids: Eerdmans, 2005), 13–20, for more on laws and norms.
6. Ray Van Leeuwen, "Liminality and Worldview in Proverbs 1–9," *Semeia* 50 (1990): 116.
7. See also Psa 111:10.
8. See also Neh 9; Pss 78; 119; Jer 4.
9. Isa 40:13; 43:10; John 17:3; Acts 17:23–31.
10. John 10:9; 14:6.
11. Matt 22:34–40; Mark 12:28–31.
12. John 3:16; 1 John 4:7–19.
13. Rom 10:4.
14. Mic 6:8.
15. This is an intentionally stark contrast to the poisonous lips of the forbidden woman of Prov 5:3; 7:5–21; 9:13–18.

Chapter 5: Putting It All Together: Kingdom, Mission, and Discipleship

1. Amy L. Sherman, *Kingdom Calling: Vocational Stewardship for the Common Good* (Downers Grove, IL: IVP Books, 2011), 100.
2. Quoted by Christopher W. Morgan and Robert A. Peterson, eds., *The Kingdom of God* (Wheaton: Crossway, 2012), 23.
3. Stephen J. Nichols, "The Kingdoms of God: The Kingdom in Historical and Contemporary Perspectives," in *The Kingdom of God*, ed. Christopher W. Morgan and Robert A. Peterson (Wheaton, IL: Crossway, 2012), 31.
4. Miroslav Volf, *Work in the Spirit: Toward a Theology of Work* (Eugene, OR: Wipf and Stock, 2001), 83.
5. Wright, *The Mission of God's People*, 25.
6. Herman Bavinck, *Our Reasonable Faith* (Grand Rapids: Eerdmans, 1956), 17.
7. Ibid., 19.
8. Greg Forster, "Theology that Works: Making Disciples who Practice Fruitful Work and Economic Wisdom in Modern America," Version 2.0 (The Oikonomia Network, 2013), 16.
9. Wolters, *Creation Regained*, 90.
10. Wolters, *Creation Regained*, 87.

Conclusion: The Way Forward

1. See appendix B for a list of such questions.
2. See appendixes A and C for a list of centers, institutes, and books.

Appendix A: With Whom Shall We Work? A Framework for Collaboration

1. Pope John XXIII, *Ad Petri Cathedram* (June 29, 1959), http://w2.vatican.va/content/john-xxiii/en/encyclicals/documents/hf_j-xxiii_enc_29061959_ad-petri.html.
2. "Catholicity" here refers to the church universal—all Christians in all times and places. It also refers to a core set of Christian doctrines (as discussed in this chapter).
3. Dorothy Sayers, "Why Work?," in *Letters to a Diminished Church*, 132.

4. David W. Miller, *God at Work: The History and Promise of the Faith at Work Movement* (Oxford: Oxford University Press, 2007), 7.

5. The term "Business as Mission" (or BAM) was coined in the early 1990s by Michael Baer, who published a book with the same title in 2006. Since he coined the phrase, however, "Business as Mission" has been borrowed and branded by many ministries and organizations attempting to integrate the Christian faith with business practices.

6. For more on Christian Chefs International, visit http://www.christianchefs.org/index.html.

7. See the notes in David W. Miller, *God at Work*, for more organizations and initiatives to this end.

8. John Armstrong, *Your Church Is Too Small* (Grand Rapids: Zondervan, 2010), 17–18.

9. Ibid., 81.

10. It should be noted that "solidarity" has an established presence in the Roman Catholic tradition and focuses on respect for all people, neighbor love, justice, and peace.

11. Martin Luther King, Jr., "Letter From A Birmingham Jail" (1963).

SUBJECT AND AUTHOR INDEX

Old Testament

New Testament